General editor: Graham Handl

Brodie's Notes on Stan Barstow's
A Kind of Loving and Joby

Philip Gooden BA
English Department, Kingswood School, Bath

Pan Books London, Sydney and Auckland

The author and Pan Books Ltd would like to
thank Stan Barstow and Michael Joseph Ltd
for permission to quote extracts from
A Kind of Loving (1960) and *Joby* (1964).

First published 1989 by Pan Books Ltd,
Cavaye Place, London SW10 9PG
9 8 7 6 5 4 3 2 1
© Pan Books Ltd 1989
ISBN 0 330 50266 2
Photoset by Parker Typesetting Service, Leicester
Printed and bound in Great Britain by
Richard Clay Ltd, Bungay, Suffolk

Contents

Preface

The intention throughout this study aid is to stimulate and guide, to encourage the reader's *involvement* in the text, to develop disciplined critical responses and a sure understanding of the main details in the chosen text.

Brodie's Notes provide a summary of the plot of the play or novel followed by act, scene or chapter summaries, each of which will have an accompanying critical commentary designed to underline the most important literary and factual details. Textual notes will be explanatory or critical (sometimes both), defining what is difficult or obscure on the one hand, or stressing points of character, style or plot on the other. Revision questions will be set on each act or group of chapters to test the student's careful application to the text of the prescribed book.

The second section of each of these study aids will consist of a critical examination of the author's art. This will cover such major elements as characterization, style, structure, setting, theme(s) or any other aspect of the book which the editor considers needs close study. The paramount aim is to send the student back to the text. Each study aid will include a series of general questions which require a detailed knowledge of the set book; the first of these questions will have notes by the editor of what *might* be included in a written answer.

Graham Handley

A Kind of Loving
Introduction

Son of a miner, Stan Barstow was born in Yorkshire in 1928 and educated at Ossett Grammar School. He achieved literary prominence with *A Kind of Loving* (first published 1960). The story of its central character and narrator, Vic Brown, was continued in *The Watchers on the Shore* (1966) and completed in *The Right True End* (1976). The first novel, however, stands by itself, and the open-ended, provisional quality of the close of *A Kind of Loving* does not demand any sequels; there is no artistic reason to supply what happens next, and this first novel in what became a trilogy is in some ways the most satisfying of the three. The book was filmed in 1962, with Alan Bates playing the central role, and all three novels were adapted by the author for television in the early 1980s. The other book studied in this guide, *Joby*, first appeared in 1964.

Barstow's work should be seen in the context, literary and social, of its period, although the continued popularity of *A Kind of Loving* of course demonstrates that its interest and appeal are much more than sociological or 'historical'. Looking back at British writing in the decade and a half or so that followed on the end of the Second World War (i.e. until the early 1960s), it is possible to see patterns and categories that may not have been apparent at the time. Equally, it is likely that novels, plays and even films, that were lumped together because they seemed then to share a common outlook or style of facing the world or a common subject-matter, were in fact more distinct from each other than appeared to critics or journalists, eager to spot a trend or identify a 'school' of writers all working along the same lines.

Barstow has been put in the regional category. Some of the other novelists associated with him are Alan Sillitoe, Keith Waterhouse and John Braine. The most famous books by these writers – respectively, *Saturday Night and Sunday Morning* (1958), *Billy Liar* (1959) and *Room at the Top* (1957) – are set in the north of England. Each has as its central male character a figure who is in some ways at odds with his environment and who does not possess the standard 'heroic' features of a protagonist. Arthur

Seaton, in *Saturday Night and Sunday Morning*, is a rebellious anti-social individual who asserts his independence from the dulling routine of factory life. He aligns himself with an old, spiky working-class tradition of antagonism towards authority, respectability and convention. Billy, in Waterhouse's *Billy Liar*, is a compulsive fantasist and liar who ultimately lacks the nerve to break away from his northern roots. Joe Lampton, the central figure in Braine's *Room at the Top*, and a man with much more regard for himself than the reader can ever have, spends his time climbing laboriously into a position where he can look down on his northern roots. What these books have in common are a shared regional background, a careful attention to the surface details of daily life, principal characters who are in some respects unsympathetic, and a directness and energy that seemed to hold out the prospect of revitalizing the English novel-writing tradition of the time. In addition, the books by Sillitoe and Braine dealt with sexual matters in a fashion that was, for their day, frank.

The general posture of these novelists, at least in the works under discussion – a posture that was restless, dissatisfied with things as they were – caused them to overlap with a slightly earlier group of authors, such as Kingsley Amis (novelist), John Osborne (playwright), Colin Wilson (essayist and novelist), whose work had caused them to be branded collectively as 'angry young men' by the media.

It should be apparent from this that the author of *A Kind of Loving* has links with these other novelists grouped in the regional school. There is, firstly, the setting, a northern industrial town, and the action, placed firmly within the families who make their living there. Vic Brown is unashamedly working class, although (as discussed in the commentary on Chapter 1) he and the other children in the Brown family have chosen, or intend to choose, occupations that will lift them out of that class. It is perhaps significant – because it demonstrates Vic's relative contentment with his status – that he is the least ambitious of the three; his sister is a teacher, his younger brother means to study medicine, while he switches from his job in the draughtsmen's office to a post in a shop. Another aspect of Barstow's work which allies him with the writers mentioned above is his focus on the surface of everyday life; its petty irritations and satisfactions, quarrels and reconciliations. And below that, the sheer physical business of working through the routine of the day, at home or at work, getting out of bed in the morning, catching the bus, having a drink in a pub, giving blood to the transfusion service. Such detail is inevitably undramatic but nonetheless interesting because it is skilfully described and because Barstow recognizes and values the importance of the routine.

Barstow's frankness over sexual matters is also echoed by the other novelists I have mentioned. The lack of reserve, the straightforwardness, with which Vic describes his feelings, his anxieties, his urges, might seem unexceptional to the present-day reader, but there is no doubt that such honesty (which is not the same as explicitness) would have struck those who read *A Kind of Loving* on its first publication. Early reviews of Sillitoe's *Saturday Night and Sunday Morning* talk about that book's 'rawness', 'freshness', lack of inhibition, and the same terms could be applied to Barstow's novel.

But *A Kind of Loving* is not a reflection or duplication of other works of the same period. The things that distinguish it from them are more significant than the similarities. Perhaps most important is the question of tone. In its depiction of a working-class family and the wider community the book is warm and sympathetic. As already indicated, Vic's attitude towards the class and environment into which he was born is one of contentment. He is a respectful, and in many ways, a conventional person. It is true that he gets dissatisfied and restless in his work as a draughtsman, but his change of job could hardly be described as the central crisis or concern of the novel.

In fact the regional and working-class setting of the novel aren't overridingly important. Vic is not obsessed with class, as Braine's 'hero' is in *Room at the Top*, nor does the novel have the subversively 'political' overtones of *Saturday Night and Sunday Morning*. This is partly because the community presented in *A Kind of Loving* is a relatively affluent one, in which it is possible for the capable or hard-working to rise through their own efforts. There is a lack of rancour or antagonism towards the social system, although there are a number of reminders by one or two of the older characters that their class had within living memory (i.e. the Depression of the 1930s) been through some tough times. The novel's background is, therefore, just that, a screen in front of which a personal drama is played out. The crisis in Vic's life, the destruction of his hopes and plans, his slow development as a character and his accommodation to reality, a coming to terms with adult life – these are events and changes which could and do happen to anyone, irrespective of geographical place, 'class', etc. If the novel still stands in its own right, as it does, then it is because of the validity and truthfulness of Barstow's recreation of the inner and outer life of his narrator, and the author's skill in persuading the reader to find common ground with his principal character. Some of the elements in the novel are universal – descriptions of family or married life and the routine of work. Other aspects, particularly the way in which Vic is forced into a 'shotgun' wedding, are more indicative of a stricter, more cramping moral climate than prevails now. What remains constant is the tangle of emotions and responses – guilt, self-reproach, bitterness, determination to make the best of things – which the narrator puts before the reader.

Barstow may not lay great stress on the provincial, working-class background in *A Kind of Loving*, and he certainly doesn't lapse into the kind of sentimentality which would portray the lives of his characters as somehow more 'real' or authentic than those of the 'sheltered' middle class. The period, however, in which the novel is set is a key factor in influencing the course of events. Although, as suggested above, the responses, confusions and anxieties of his characters are not particular to one time or place, the fact remains that the narrative of *A Kind of Loving* would not take the course it does if the book were set in the present day. His characters are in part conditioned by their time – as we all are.

It is plain that events unfold – just – before the so-called permissive period of the 1960s. The attitude of the two families, Browns and Rothwells, is fixed: pleasures, or foolish behaviour, have to be paid for; an unwanted pregnancy entails an unwanted marriage. Vic himself implicitly endorses this attitude. He has to do the 'right thing', partly because his conscience demands it and partly because nobody expects him to do otherwise. Indeed, everybody whose opinion he respects would be outraged were he to attempt to back out of his responsibilities. He complains about the bad luck that has landed him where he doesn't want to be, but he doesn't question or rebel against the moral and social expectations of his family and community since to a large extent he shares those expectations.

It might be claimed that there is implicit criticism of a moral/ social system which more or less forced two young people together, after one 'slip up' and irrespective of their true feelings for each other. When Vic is looking for sympathy from his sister he tells her, 'It doesn't matter whether you love her [that is, the girl who gets pregnant before marriage] or not as long as you make her respectable.' The comment is angry but it represents all that he has to say by way of attack on the code of conduct that directs his life. And although the word 'respectable' in the quotation above must be delivered with cynicism or bitterness, Vic's words and actions elsewhere in the novel show that he does in fact place a high premium on 'respectability'. His parents epitomize it. When he eventually returns to Ingrid at the end he is able to regain his self-esteem and win back 'respectability' in the eyes of the two families. But the former is the more important.

A Kind of Loving does not, therefore, offer a critique of, or an assault on the conventional sexual morality of the period. Vic's problem is less that he is forced into a marriage than that he is compelled to marry a woman he does not love. And his feelings towards her have nothing to do with the morality or conventions of the period, which may seem to the modern reader a little dated. The type of relationship that is evolving between Vic and Ingrid at the end of the book is perhaps more recognizable, and is one of the things that make *A Kind of Loving* into a literary bridge between the spirit of the 1950s and the 1960s. Vic and Ingrid commit themselves to each other, but it is a private and provisional act. Nothing holds them together, except a sort of willingness to see whether matters might work out all right. She loves him, he is doing 'the right thing' (but for himself rather than others), the future is far from assured. All they can do is their best. As suggested in the commentary on Chapter 1, we can interpret this reunion as a counterpart to the more formal union (of Chris and David) celebrated at the novel's opening. The older couple are matched for life, their commitment to each other is absolute, as Vic sees. But the younger pair are tentative, far from sure of themselves or what's to come. In this respect at least the novel could be considered very much of our times.

Another aspect which marks out *A Kind of Loving* as dealing with a transitional period in society, one in which the austerity of the post-war era was being replaced with a culture of consumer affluence, is the frequency with which some (older) characters contrast past and present. The changes of the 1950s were considerable, and mostly material ones. At the start of the decade few households had a television; food rationing (a result of the war) was still in existence; the average weekly wage was £8.30 for men. By the end of the decade – the date of the first publication of Barstow's novel – every statistic signalled growing prosperity, and most households (particularly working-class ones) were experiencing unprecedented material well-being. As the old miner tells Mr Brown and Vic in the pub, 'We've never had it as good as this last ten year'; as Uncle William tells Vic's father, with only a touch of mockery, he is one of the 'new aristocracy, living off the fat o' the land, sending your lad to college to study medicine'. In some of the older generation this relatively recent affluence produces the fear that all that they've gained will be as speedily taken away. For members of the younger generation like Vic or Conroy, however, such prosperity is taken for granted. There are plenty of jobs ('T'evenin' paper's allus full o' vacancies for draughtsmen', says Mr Brown); work is rewarded with 'a decent livin' wage'; Vic can make a joke about going on the dole, because it is not something he has ever considered as a possibility.

This material comfort does not make for recklessness or extravagance. There is no surplus, of money, of possessions, but there is – and perhaps for the first time in the working-class experience – enough for most families or individuals. *A Kind of Loving* comes at the end of the first stage of British post-war development, when general affluence was still sufficiently novel to be commented on.

Such new-found prosperity is significant in Barstow's work, not only because of the individual slant it gives to a statistical truth, but because it does seem to underpin or shape the attitudes and actions of some of the characters. Conroy can be rude towards his superior in the Drawing Office since getting the sack doesn't matter to him; there are plenty of other openings for his skills. There is full employment. Business is booming. Vic does his bit here by putting his energy and wits into the reorganizing of Mr Van Huyten's old-fashioned record shop. The younger man can see the necessity for new ideas, more aggressive and imaginative selling, competition. He works not so much for personal profit as for the satisfaction of doing good business. In his dedication to this – 'It nigh breaks my heart to think of the shop being shut and all that trade being turned away', he thinks at one point – and in his confident belief that success is there to be seized, Vic embodies the mood of expansive assurance that characterized a country finally pulling out of the doldrums of economic and social inertia.

A Kind of Loving – chapter commentaries, textual notes, revision questions and assignments

Part One
Chapter 1

The opening chapter covers a single, notable day in the life of Vic Brown, the narrator and central character of *A Kind of Loving*. It is the day of his sister's wedding and 'the day I decided to *do* something about Ingrid Rothwell besides gawp at her like a love-sick cow'.

The family celebration and the narrator's decision to be more assertive in his pursuit of Ingrid are related, and not merely in the sense that his sister's marriage prompts Vic to consider the kind of relationship, the kind of girl, that he wants. The novel begins with a marriage of a traditional type. Barstow effectively conveys the anxieties, the little panics, the humour, the warmth, the family bickerings that belong to such an occasion. But we are left in no doubt that this is a union between two people who are well matched. It is a union that is thoroughly approved of by the bride's family; even Vic, who idealizes his sister and might therefore be expected to feel that any husband wouldn't be good enough for her, is 'real happy for them ... because David's a good bloke'.

Much of the rest of the novel is devoted to charting the relationship between Vic and Ingrid. She becomes pregnant; they marry; their situation worsens with her miscarriage and the couple's being forced to live with Ingrid's parents; eventually, and after scenes of bitter disagreement, Vic and his wife resolve to start again in the hope that 'we might find a kind of loving to carry us through' (see final chapter). In a sense the book could be said to end as it begins, with a marriage, but this time there is no jubilation and little confidence about the future. It is as if Barstow were presenting the reader with the ideal, the union of Chris and David, as witnessed from outside, and contrasting it with the reality, the often ragged relationship between Vic and Ingrid, as experienced from the inside. There is, too, something recognizably more 'modern' in the provisional quality of the union of Vic and Ingrid. By contrast the marriage with which the novel opens, a marriage made for life between perfectly suited partners, may strike us, for better or worse, as being optimistic (and old-fashioned?) in its hopeful commitment.

In narrative terms, the wedding is a convenient device enabling the author to introduce at one go all the significant figures in Vic's family. A wedding, like a funeral, overrides the everyday, and can both soothe and aggravate family tensions – in either event it provides good material for the novelist and, as here, a useful starting point. Vic's family is close-knit. The celebration of this chapter highlights the harmonious ties that bind its members. Vic views them differently – respect and mockery mingle in his treatment of his younger brother, Jim 'the scholar'; there is impatience as well as admiration in his attitude towards his father. At the root of his feelings, however, are affection and tolerance. There is a marked lack of tension between the members of this family and each individual seems secure of his or her position within the family circle. The Browns are presented as robust, warm-hearted, unostentatious, fundamentally content. They are not static, though. The children are travelling down paths that were not open to the parents. The older generation is working-class (Vic's father is a pit deputy, his uncle is foreman at an engineering works). The younger generation is moving towards the middle class: Chris is a teacher, Vic a draughtsman, his younger brother has ambitions to become a doctor. This change in social status causes no resentment or friction between the generations. The parents, in particular the 'Old Lady', take pride in the achievements of their children. (See Introduction for further discussion of this topic.)

The character we learn most about in the opening chapter is Vic Brown, the narrator. This isn't because he is immodest or self-centred. It is rather that, in a first person narration, we discover things about the story-teller partly from what he chooses to reveal about himself but also from what he chooses to reveal about others. Even when the subject is not ostensibly himself (as it is when Vic describes his appearance and something of his character at the beginning of section IV in this chapter) the narrator is generally telling us something – of his tastes, prejudices, mood, etc. – by his selection of detail and emphasis in his description of people or events. An example of this occurs in Chapter 1 when Vic describes his brother Jim, the 'intellectual' of the family. Vic's amused respect for him suggests that he has a modest assessment of his own mental abilities, and this modesty, this sense of his own ordinariness, is one of the attractive and engaging features of his personality. It is, of course, especially important that we should experience some sympathy with the narrator in this type of personal history because we see what happens in the next three hundred or so pages through his eyes only. His failure to gain our attention, interest, sympathy would mean that the book failed.

Even when the narrator is acting as an apparently 'neutral' reporter he may in fact be giving us further information about himself. Take again the example mentioned above, Vic's attitude towards his younger brother. He goes to borrow a tie from Jim and helps him with a maths problem (section IV). This scene is almost entirely in dialogue and it confirms not only the easy bantering relationship between the brothers but tells us that Vic isn't the intellectual inferior to Jim that he considers himself to be. He hasn't the pretension to think of himself as a 'scholar', but it's obvious that he's no fool. The subtlety of this portrait of a man who is in many ways quite average – 'one of the lads', but not so lacking in self-esteem that he can't judge himself to be 'as presentable as the next bloke' – lies in the way that we as readers have to deduce Vic's qualities not just from what he says directly about himself but from his attitude to others and from dialogue which we accept as 'true' because it seems to be independent of the narrator. Barstow develops his principal character by mingling Vic's awareness of himself with his awareness of and participation in the world outside himself.

A final example taken from this chapter, and one of particular significance given the preoccupations of A Kind of Loving, concerns Vic's attitude towards sex, love and marriage. As already noted, his sister's marriage prompts thoughts of his own future partner. He has an ideal vision of a perfect partner. But as far as his friends know, his interest in women is exclusively sexual, a matter of 'cocky talk and dirty jokes and wisecracks'. Inwardly Vic is more fastidious and uncertain than he can afford to appear to his mates. We glimpse one man in the commentary that he provides upon himself, we see a different man in the bar with 'the lads'. The complexity, or confusion, of his feelings is dramatized rather than being spelled out for us.

the Great Metropolis London.

**He still thinks in terms of wages at three pound ten a week and suits
fifty bob apiece off the peg** An early indication that the generation to
which Vic belongs has higher material expectations than his parents'.
The mildly exasperated or scornful tone of the remark also suggests
that Vic has distanced himself a little from the traditional working-
class outlook of his father ('fifty bob' = about £2.50).

Is she after marrying me off next? The irony is obvious. When it
comes to Vic's marriage the 'Old Lady' can show little enthusiasm.

butcher's (hook) Look (rhyming slang).

I'm always kind of half-looking for this girl I'm going to find one day
The vagueness and tentativeness of the phrasing ('kind of half-
looking') may suggest that Vic is unwilling to put the full extent of his
romantic aspirations into words, even to himself – as if he were
embarrassed to catch himself thinking like this.

t'next wedding in the family somebody else pays for The meaning
intended by Vic's mother is that future weddings in the family will not
be at their expense (because Vic and his brother remain to be married
and it is customary for the bride's family to pay the wedding
expenses). However, the remark has ironic undertones: everyone will
'pay' (but not in a financial sense) for the marriage of Vic and Ingrid at
the end of the novel.

'not a bit o'side with it' i.e. lacking pretension or self-importance.

'a decent livin' wage' The comment reflects a new-found sense of
working-class prosperity, as experienced by a member of the older
generation who has been through the hardships of pre-war Britain.

now I feel all empty and let down with disappointment Vic's failure to
find Ingrid at the dance-hall, and the frustration of what he'd hoped
for, perhaps indicate something of the larger pattern of the novel,
where the narrator has to come to terms with disillusionment, to live
with reality rather than dreams.

Chapter 2

In the previous chapter we saw Vic's home and learned of his
private feelings about Ingrid. The second chapter describes his
workplace and the couple's first date. There is nothing sensa-
tional or overtly dramatic about what happens here. Indeed,
from the outside, the events of this and other chapters might be
described as humdrum. The very ordinariness of the daily life,
at home or at work, described in the novel contributes to its
conviction and realism. The characters live in a world of routine,
conversation that is often banal, small comforts and irritations,
the embarrassment of not having enough money to pay your bus

fare, the nice calculation about which cinema seats to buy so as to give the right impression to a girl.

The routine of others' lives has an intrinsic interest, as in those newspaper articles on 'A Day in the Life' of someone well-known. But routine by itself generally isn't enough to sustain an entire novel. Something needs to happen to disrupt that routine, as indeed it does later in *A Kind of Loving* when Vic's involvement with Ingrid turns out badly for both of them. Most of our interest in the principal character, however, stems not so much from what he does or what happens to him, but from the character himself. It is through Vic's narration that we experience, at second hand, what occurs, and although his life may be quite ordinary he feels the inner anxieties and excitements experienced by everyone. We want to see how he feels, how he copes, becauses we have been in – or can easily imagine ourselves in – similar situations. To this end it is very necessary that we should trust and like the narrator (as already suggested in the Commentary on Chapter 1). A picture of the narrator is slowly built up, at home, at work, in love – he is emerging as an honest, good-humoured man of greater sensitivity than he lets appear on the surface.

Vic's encounters with others helps to define him, as well as providing vivid little character sketches. He is tolerant of the bore on the bus partly because 'I can shut myself off by thinking about Ingrid'. But with a colleague at work who shows off his superior cultural taste by boasting of the French films he has seen, Vic is direct and abrasive, so determined to avoid joining in a game of intellectual snobbery that he presents himself as 'just another cloth-head'. The most important encounter in the chapter is with Ingrid. The mixture of timidity, excitement, apprehension, awkwardness, is rendered by Barstow with accuracy and humour. The gap between Vic's real feelings and the things he talks about with Ingrid (weather, films) is comic and true to life. The real excitement, the real drama, is taking place inside him.

D.O. Drawing office.
I quite like both the office and the work Vic'a rather lukewarm feelings about his work prepare us for his move later in the novel.
'Based on a novel by Zola' Rawlinson is trying to impress, but the more he tries the further Vic retreats into humorous display of ignorance.

Zola (1840–1902) was a nineteenth-century French writer of social and
moral conscience and power.

But that's not the way I feel about Ingrid Repeatedly Vic assures
himself that his feelings for Ingrid are too complex and high-minded
to be straightforwardly sexual.

a collier's coal supply The free quantity of coal which a miner was
entitled to receive.

Chapter 3

In the first part of this chapter we learn more about the narrator
in his working life while, in the second half, there is a further
instalment describing the lack of progress in his relationship
with Ingrid – going unsteady, as it were.

Vic's Saturday job is at a record and music shop. The
conservatism of the owner, Mr Van Huyten, 'a distinguished old
gent' for whom Vic has a genuine affection and respect, and the
gloomy attitude of the other assistant, mean that Vic has
opportunities to demonstrate his energy and initiative. He is
buoyant, optimistic, full of ideas as to how the business can be
improved – not so much for personal profit as out of pleasure in
innovation and in gaining the approval and trust of his
employer. He is contrasted with Henry, the assistant, tied to 'a
fat wife and five snotty-nosed kids', pleased to be miserable
about the future and waiting for the day when the fool's
paradise of workers' prosperity falls to pieces. There is some
irony in this. Vic himself will soon be trapped in marriage; his
pity for his fellow-worker will turn to self-pity. But Vic also
embodies in his confidence, his inventiveness, his belief in the
possibility of change for the better, the sense of expansiveness
that spread throughout Britain in the later 1950s and early
1960s, after years of war-time and post-war bleakness and
shortage.

Barstow's method of dealing with the minor characters is well
shown in this chapter. Since they are glimpsed, like everything
in *A Kind of Loving*, through the eyes of the narrator, there is
nothing formal, contrived, 'literary', about these portraits. Vic's
style – apparently casual and rambling, filled with slang – is to
select one or two details: Mr Van Huyten's chain-smoking and
the white handkerchief 'that hangs half out of his top pocket';
Dorothy (Ingrid's friend) with her 'mouth like a crack in a pie'.
Such details may point, simply, economically, to aspects of

personality. Mr Van Huyten dresses like a 'gent' and has corres-
ponding manners and qualities which Vic values highly. On the
other hand, Dorothy is an ugly intruder into his friendship with
Ingrid, and her escorting of Ingrid on what Vic hoped would be
a private walk frustrates him. It shows in his description of her
and in his crude dismissal after she has tried to drive a wedge
between Vic and Ingrid in her jealousy. The progress of their
relationship is slow; it see-saws; at the end of this chapter Vic is
down in the dumps.

**'You're not to big for a good slap, y'know, even if you are at the
shavin' stage . . .'** The remark indicates not only that the 'Old Lady'
rules her household (Vic is right to be wary of her) but that her son
hasn't yet achieved a fully adult status, in her eyes or his own. The fact
that Vic's father fixed him up with the job at the record shop, given
later in this chapter, also suggests that the young man still depends
heavily on his parents and can't act freely for himself.

I sometimes think this is the kind of job I'm cut out for. A remark
paving the way for Vic's later change of job.

'Dole?' he says. 'You ask your dad about the dole, lad.' The comment
exposes one of the things dividing Vic's generation from that of men
like his father and Henry: the younger generation has no experience
of unemployment or insecurity at work. The period in which the book
is set was one of expansion and relative working-class prosperity. Fears
of unemployment and the dole, however, haunt the older men.

Job's comforter Someone who, in attempting to bring comfort,
actually makes a situation worse.

Questions and assignments on Chapters 1–3

1 Describe the characters of the principal members of the
Brown family (parents and children) as we see them in
Chapter 1. Use quotation.

2 'Vic Brown is a more complex character than he allows
himself to appear on the surface.' Discuss what you think is
meant by this comment.

Assignments

1 The novel begins with a wedding, an occasion (like a funeral)
when the strengths and the stresses of life in a family may show
through. Write about your own experience and observations at

either a wedding or a funeral. Provide a made-up account, if you prefer.

2 Close attention is given in this novel to the small detail of everyday life – cleaning a pair of shoes, getting out of bed on a cold morning. Select a couple of such moments in your daily routine and write about them so as to bring them to fresh and accurate life.

3 Relations between the sexes are a key subject of *A Kind of Loving*. Vic is evidently less assured within himself than his outward manner and predatory style ('if you're hunting in pairs . . .') would indicate. Either from your own experience or from your observation how truthful a picture does this seem to you? For writing or discussion.

Chapter 4

Vic Brown is obsessed with Ingrid. After the fiasco of their last outing he is jubilant when, at the end of this chapter, she agrees to go out with him again. Barstow is charting in the first part of the novel the little fluctuations in Vic's emotional temperature. A terse letter plunges him into gloom, her unenthusiastic acceptance of his invitation restores him to life. Tiny things matter. He becomes very sensitive about the crude insinuations of other workers in his office and there is nearly a fight. He shrivels with embarrassment when a casual reference is made to the letter from Ingrid. Vic is obviously in love. In his own mind he is careful to distinguish between love and sex; the second without the first is, he considers, just 'biology'. Sexually inexperienced, he looks for an amalgamation of the two in his ideal relationship.

There are various encounters in this chapter. He delivers a message to the office chief, who is off sick, and he is alarmed by Hassop's sister. Later he meets an old school acquaintance in a café. Further on, other characters in Vic's office are introduced. There is a random, arbitrary quality about some of these events or encounters. *A Kind of Loving* is not a tightly organized novel in which every incident and character has a thematic or symbolic significance. Of course our impression of the narrator as a down-to-earth average man is enlarged by what he does, whom he sees and talks with, and every fresh situation and new character consolidates the 'world' of the novel, makes it more rounded.

But, as in life, some things are less important or meaningful than others. Meetings and events of no particular significance jostle moments of crisis or delight. So, during a period when Vic is completely preoccupied with thoughts of Ingrid, he meets a couple of characters – Hassop's sister, a school friend – who do not appear to have any function outside their mere existence. They could be said to be there simply to 'populate' the novel. They are, in a sense, 'accidents', not serving some higher purpose of the writer. There is a mild mystery surrounding the circumstances of Hassop's home life, but it's never cleared up. Similarly, in reality, we all come across puzzles and oddities in the actions and behaviour of others (as well as in ourselves!) which have to remain unexplained.

phizzog Face (old slang).

I reckon there'll be right 'uns and wrong 'uns among them like there is with anybody else. Vic's comments on the immigrant population of the town show tolerance and fair-mindedness. Racial discrimination was as common in the period in which *A Kind of Loving* is set (the late 1950s) as in later decades. The mild curiosity and basic decency of his attitude are characteristic.

God! I'm glad I'm English. Not to be read as the expression of some mindless patriotism, the exclamation reflects Vic's consciousness of his comparative good fortune. His straightforward attachment to his country is very different from the despair or hatred expressed by the central figures (sometimes referred to as 'anti-heroes') in other novels and plays of this period.

gyp Pain (slang).

'A grammar school lad drilling lumps o' metal.' The remark illustrates how widespread was the belief that certain types of schooling fitted you for certain jobs; a 'grammar school lad', and therefore by definition academically able, ought to be wearing 'a collar an' tie' (i.e. have an office job, like Vic). In fact Jackson prefers to work with his hands. Vic's words indicate a rather conventional acceptance of a whole set of assumptions to do with education, class, status and work.

although I don't like Conroy any more than I like Rawly I think it's a very smart remark Vic has been interested by what Rawlinson has said but is glad when a slightly crude remark from Conroy deflates him, because Rawlinson uses 'culture' as a means of establishing his superiority to the other office workers. On the other hand, Vic finds Conroy's coarseness offensive when it's applied to the subject of Ingrid a little later in this chapter.

Chapter 5

The relationship between Vic and Ingrid reaches a new intensity in this chapter but Barstow hints at the same time at some of the things that will eventually drive a wedge between them. The first section of the chapter is Vic's account of how he was stood up by Ingrid only to discover when he returned home, disappointed, that she has written him a letter apologizing for not meeting him and arranging another rendezvous. His mood swings from despair to delight. In the park with her he is overcome by gratitude and physical excitement, all doubts swept away.

But the doubts do exist, and they are faintly ominous pointers to the future. The couple don't have the same tastes. Ingrid says 'she can't read books'. Vic is not well-read, as his brother-in-law David is, but he is curious to learn more and considers that there is 'something just in the *feel* of a book ... something solid that's here to stay'. He has a mild contempt for those whose only entertainment is the 'telly'. This is a small indication of the gap between the couple but it does spoil a little his vision of their perfect future harmony. Vic's interest in books, like his fondness for music, is one of the things that link him to his brother and sister, with their aspirations and desire to broaden their horizons, and that separate him from the world of his parents.

His attitude to sex is troubled. He is guilty and uneasy when his mother questions him about his friendship with Ingrid. The Old Lady would see it as 'something shabby and dirty'. At one level Vic feels that this would be a gross misrepresentation; the experience for him was transformed by love and gratitude. At another level, however, he shares what he believes would be his mother's instinctive response: that sex is necessary but somehow regrettable, and that to admit to enjoying it is shameful, putting you in the same class 'as drunkards and gamblers'. From this point onward in the novel Vic is perturbed by a confusion of feelings. Every stage of the growing sexual intimacy of himself and Ingrid is stamped with guilt – a guilt that is partly the product of his background and upbringing, for we can take the slightly puritanical outlook of his mother as being representative of the attitude not merely of the middle-aged working-class generation but also of the whole climate of opinion which prevailed in relation to sexual morality in England during the 1950s. We should note also that Vic's confusion springs from a certain fastidiousness in his nature. When, at the end of this chapter, he is arguing in his head with what he thinks his mother would say if she knew what had occurred in the park, asserting that 'it wasn't like that [i.e. something shabby and dirty] at all', he is arguing with himself. Sex, which by itself is no more than 'biology', is only redeemed by love.

'Boners' noses' Joke version of the Spanish for goodnight, *buenas noches*.

Ulysses The famous novel by James Joyce (1882–1941). *Ulysses* was first published in Paris in 1922 and immediately banned in Britain and America on the grounds of obscenity. The part which Vic is skimming through in the copy taken from David's shelves and which shocks him by its sexual frankness is the final section of the novel, a long and completely unpunctuated monlogue by Molly Bloom, the novel's principal female character. *Ulysses* – 'one of the most significant books in the language', as David points out in his teacherly fashion – became notorious for its 'dirty bits', of which Molly's helter-skelter night thoughts are perhaps the most notorious. Vic is concerned in case his sister should see it, and although this reaction might seem rather prudish to us it is typical of the more guarded period in which *A Kind of Loving* is set.

Raymond Chandler The American writer (1888–1959) who gave a literary gloss and style to the private-eye story that lifted the status of the US crime novel and made it academically respectable.

For Whom the Bell Tolls Novel by Ernest Hemingway (1899–1961), based on the author's own first-hand experience of the Spanish Civil War. Vic's own taste in books is unpretentious but he is willing to be taught more by his brother-in-law.

I notice the way she says 'mother' . . . and this puts her family a notch above mine straight away Vic is sensitive to the subtle gradations of the class system in which divisions are marked at least as much by the way things are phrased as by possessions held or money earned. Similarly, the slight distance which Vic has moved from his parents – because of his education and the (office) job he now holds – is registered by the fact that his speech is less marked by dialect and is closer to 'standard' English than the Old Feller's.

Just the way I want it: living and loving and laughing together, every day Ingrid's hopes for her marriage coincide with Vic's own vision. Given what happens to them there is perhaps some irony in this, but there is also a touching quality to his hopefulness. There isn't a trace of cynicism here.

I think it's a pity she doesn't read Having reached a new understanding with Ingrid, and after clearing up past misunderstandings, Vic implicitly considers their relationship as a long-term one – one in which they could have shared an interest in reading.

Chapter 6

For the first time since the beginning of the novel Vic's preoccupation with Ingrid fades into the background. It is significant that, although seeing her often now, he feels that 'there isn't the magic there was'. He can no longer envisage her as the woman who might be his wife. Two other narrative strands run through this chapter. There is a fight in the office between Vic and Conroy, which results in the two being summoned by the boss. Vic sees a new side to Conroy's aggressive hard-edged manner, an almost admirable readiness to stand up to any man. The second section of the chapter underlines the warmth and affection at the heart of the Brown family. Despite differences in outlook between the generations and despite the Old Lady's habit of treating Vic sometimes as a child, there is no doubting the closeness and strength of the family bonds.

(Conroy) not knuckling under at all to what Althorpe's saying While Vic is silent and subdued at his employer's rebuke, Conroy is argumentative and stubborn. Vic is too respectful of his superiors to behave like this but Conroy rises in his estimation; at the same time he thinks the less of Althorpe because of the crude language used by someone of his father's age and authority.

'I reckon this is all my fault for cracking at you the way I did' The two men are, temporarily, allies because they have both been reprimanded by Althorpe. The remark registers the new-found respect Vic has for his fellow-worker.

Probably married, maybe with some kids. But who to? Who would the bint be? Vic's speculation are not particularly urgent. He expects to get married and have children, in the normal course of events. The revealing part of this standard vision of the future is that Ingrid plays no part in it. Knowing her better, he no longer sees her as an ideal partner.

National Service In 1948 the government instituted a system of compulsory military training and service for young men for a two-year period. Those in certain occupations got their service deferred. As Vic suggests in his conversation with his father, he half regrets not having been called up. His father sees military service as futile, a disruption of a young man's career. National Service was abolished in 1960, the year in which *A Kind of Loving* first appeared.

I'm surprised because it's never occurred to me he might be proud of me A mark of Vic's modesty; he doesn't see himself as a 'scholar' like his brother or an achiever like his sister. Nevertheless, in his father's view, Vic's job as a draughtsman is an escape from the work he would

otherwise have been forced into at the pit, as well as a badge of status
in its own right.

'This is a golden age for young fowk' It is a golden age because young
people are no longer compelled to enter one of only two occupations
('pit or t'mills'), because they have choice, more money, and better
working conditions. At the same time Mr Brown's friend, Herbert,
expresses a faint contempt for the 'softness' of workers of his son's
generation. This contrast between the working lives and expectations
of the two generations is one of the minor concerns of the novel. A
more up-to-date attitude to work is embodied in Conroy at the
beginning of this chapter. A skilled craftsman, he can afford to stand
up to his employer. If he loses one job he can easily find another. Such
an attitude – carefree, almost rebellious – would have horrified older
workers who lived in constant fear that the 'boom' period of the late
1950s onwards would come to an end. Indeed, just such a point of
view is voiced later on in this conversation. A slump, loss of jobs and
hard times – all these were always in prospect, for those old enough to
remember the 1930s and of a gloomy turn of mind.

Chapter 7

This chapter, the end of the first half of the novel, is also the end
of the affair with Ingrid as far as Vic is concerned. Ironically,
once they have reached a stage of physical intimacy which is
almost the same as 'going all the way', Vic realizes all the things
that separate them. In a mood of self-disgust, he begins to
catalogue the irritating aspects of her conversation and
behaviour: her liking for gossip and scandal, even the way she
puts on her make-up. He can now only find fault with the
woman he idolized a few weeks previously. He has dropped out
of love as fast as he fell into it. He sees himself as the victim of a
sexual impulse which, until satisfied, has disguised from him the
essential incompatibility between Ingrid and himself. 'Sex and a
dream' have got confused inside him and once one desire is
fulfilled he understands, with painful clear sight, how remote
Ingrid is from fulfilling any of his more high-minded requirements in a partner.

It might be objected that this account is very one-sided. Ingrid
is as much a victim of her feelings as Vic is of his. Her only 'fault'
is to have been compliant to his desires; she is hardly to blame if
her interests are somehow less 'intellectual' than his. All these
points are true; the story would have been very different if it
had been told through her eyes. But the narrator is male and it is

his outlook and responses that we are invited to identify or sympathize with. Vic presents his disillusionment with Ingrid as something beyond his control – 'you can't help the way you feel, can you?' – and while there is an element of self-justification here there is also a genuine bafflement at the way his emotions have swung from one extreme to another. Unable to understand himself, he cannot see how to explain things to her. He has some regard for her feelings, and hopes that he can ease himself out of the relationship by evasion and excuses rather than by a direct confrontation. This may not put him in a very attractive or admirable light but Vic is not an unusual or exceptional figure, and his wish to end the friendship by the least painful means is both realistic and understandable.

a twinge of guilt The inescapable association of sex and guilt is again stressed.
She gave me the green light okay Vic is trying to transfer some of the 'blame' for what has happened. It is Ingrid's fault as much as his.
I've lost something tonight, and to a lass I don't much like, let alone love He has lost his self-respect, because he has given way to a sexual urge quite divorced from love. In this way he has denied his own innermost ambitions.

Questions and assignments on Chapters 4–7

1 Describe carefully the development of Vic's relationship with Ingrid in these chapters. Try to account for the changes of mood which Vic experiences.

2 Barstow shows that his characters have different attitudes towards the work that they do, whether in a mine or in a draughtsman's office. Describe and discuss some of these different attitudes.

Assignments

1 Write a dialogue between a member of the older working generation and a younger one in which they discuss their present working lives and hopes or fears for the future, using whatever evidence you can find in these chapters.

2 Take any episode involving Ingrid from this section of the novel and re-describe it from her point of view. Include as many of her thoughts and feelings as possible.

3 Vic describes the community of his place of work – its tensions and humour. Write about your experience of a working community (which could include a school) in a similar way.

Part Two
Chapter 1

The relationship with Ingrid, which Vic had determined to finish, is resumed. But the complexity of his feelings in the first part of the novel has narrowed and simplified. There's no longer any love involved on Vic's part; instead 'now I want her like I want the bints in the magazines. It's not really *her* I want at all, if you see what I mean.' Desire is followed by a sense of shame and guilt, and then the attempt at self-justification. Vic tells himself that he is somehow acting in the way that Ingrid would prefer – 'she'd rather have me this way than not at all'. The relationship, for him reduced to a level which is almost exclusively sexual, gets relegated to a corner of his life. In fact the strongest emotion Vic experiences in this chapter is not to do with Ingrid at all, but with the departure of Conroy from the Drawing Office. Vic has just begun to get to know the man, to penetrate his crude exterior and realize the presence beneath of a more sensitive and complicated individual. Vic responds to Conroy's taking him into his confidence (the latter tells him he has been married), and both men have a similiar distrust of 'fakes' like Rawlinson who make a great display of their cultural superiority. There is an affinity between the two in that both present to the world images of themselves that are appropriate to a society dominated by simple male values: Vic is 'one of the lads', Conroy is loud-mouthed, assertive, impudent. But there is another side to their characters. Vic already knows his own 'secrets'; he is surprised to discover the hidden aspects of his fellow-worker. He is disappointed to lose the company of a man who might have become a good friend.

M.C. Master of Ceremonies.
'It's not whether I liked it or not that matters,' Rawly says, real distant like; 'but what the management thinks.' The comment shows Rawlinson in a very unfavourable light. His stiff, 'correct' personality

is implicitly contrasted with Conroy's spontaneity and directness. Rawlinson is always concerned to make the right impression; Conroy seems to go out of his way to leave the wrong one, to show that he is not deferential to the opinions of others (particularly 'the management').

Debussy French composer (1862–1918).

Dostoyevsky Russian novelist (1821–81), author of *Crime and Punishment*.

Tolstoy Russian novelist (1828–1910), author of *War and Peace* and *Anna Karenina*. According to Conroy, a fake like Rawlinson uses the names of writers and composers as counters in a game of cultural one-upmanship. He doesn't really know much. Conroy, on the other hand, without boasting about it, is genuinely knowledgeable.

'I reckon you're getting summat you won't get out of *Peg's Paper* and last week's Top Ten' The comment by Conroy is an echo of Vic's own thoughts at an earlier point, when he compares the 'solid' quality of a book to the less satisfactory rewards of watching 'telly'.

Conroy's a Highbrow i.e. someone with a taste for 'difficult' writers, composers, etc., not read or listened to by the general public.

I remember how I felt after last time, but somehow it seems different now, and I can't think about that Vic's scruples about getting involved with Ingrid again disappear. Touching her on the dance-floor, embracing in the car – sex outweighs caution.

Nil illegitimum (carborundum) Piece of advice expressed in joke Latin, and 'translated' by Conroy for Vic.

I wonder if a change of job mightn't do *me* good Conroy's departure underlines Vic's restlessness.

It's a mess Vic's description of the state of his affair with Ingrid could be interpreted as a further piece of self-justification since it suggests he finds himself in a situation beyond his control – but it's a 'mess' that brings him some pleasures, even if they are followed by a mood of impatience or self-disgust.

Chapter 2

Victor changes his job. The move has been prepared for by the author: Vic's restlessness has been stressed, as has the enthusiasm he brings to suggesting innovations in the record shop where he now takes up full-time work. Mr Van Huyten's trust and affection touch Vic, and after careful discussion with his parents – their approval (almost their consent) is vital to his decision – he leaves Whittaker's. Just before he goes, Ingrid has an accident; she falls downstairs (a foreshadowing of the more serious incident in Chapter 7), and the coincidence of her being out of the way and off work at the same time as Vic is leaving the firm give him the opportunity to 'break off properly, for good'. It can be a painless separation because he will not have to confront her again. Chance and circumstances seem to be arranging his life in the shape that he really wants – terminating his involvement with the girl and his job in the Drawing Office at the same moment – and he feels happy enough to go along with events when they are working out to his advantage, like most of us.

Brahms German composer (1833–97). Barstow doesn't overplay the 'sensitive' side of Vic's nature. Unlike Conroy, the narrator does not reveal a sudden and surprising capacity for aesthetic appreciation. He is bored by Brahms.

I'm touched, and when I remember the dates with Ingrid I'm a bit ashamed as well Vic is ashamed because he thinks less well of himself than Mr Van Huyten does. In his own eyes he is not so trustworthy, honourable, etc., as the old man supposes him to be.

'I think happen I'd better have a word with him,' the Old Feller says It is interesting to note the attitudes of son and parents here. Mr Brown expects to discuss Vic's change of job with his new employer. The way in which it is referred to at the start of the next section – 'A week later it's all settled' – almost suggests that the matter is out of Vic's hands, that he did not have the final say in whether he would move from Whittaker's. Nor does the son appear to resent the role of the father; Vic's expectation that the Old Feller will settle things is not merely a telling reminder of the different social and family traditions that prevailed more than a quarter of a century ago but also indicates the essentially conformist, conventional nature of Vic's outlook. When it comes to the question of marriage the parents will demand an even stronger say.

I'm glad she can't write because it means she can't pin me down The mild selfishness of the thought is realistic enough. The 'convenience' of the injury is that it will make communication between the two difficult, and so Vic will be able to slip more comfortably out of a relationship which he is evidently finding oppressive (the phrase 'pin me down' is revealing).

Chapter 3

Against his better judgement Vic once again finds himself entangled with Ingrid. When she comes into the record shop with the obvious intention of resuming the affair, Vic, swept away by excitement, agrees to meet her again. The familiar cycle of desire and guilt is re-established, but its very routineness dulls

Vic so that it takes something out of the ordinary – like her giving him a twenty-first birthday present – to affect him on an emotional rather than a physical level. The atmosphere of the couple's meetings is cold. By tacit agreement they do not refer to love. Instead their encounters are speckled with little disagreements (such as the one over Vic's giving money to a tramp in a cafe), small areas of dislike (he objects to the way she holds her coffee cup). All this is trivial but it is symptomatic of the coolness between the two, their ultimate incompatibility. Barstow merely 'records' here, reproduces the small talk, the petty differences, but the chapter as a whole gives us an image of a man and a woman trapped in a relationship which neither of them is much enjoying but which neither can break away from. The 'documentary' style of the novel, the feeling we have that we are witnessing a sequence of events that is plausible and uncontrived, make it difficult to moralize or pass judgement. The author is not 'for' or 'against' any particular character (except a minor figure such as Rawlinson), although in a first-person narrative there is an inevitable pressure on the reader to identify to an extent with the individual telling the story. We may not consider that the central character is behaving particularly well or sensibly here, and in this context it is significant that it is Ingrid rather than he who initiates the resumption of their relationship. But such considerations are secondary to the principal demands that the novel makes on us: that we should see here a recognizable picture of ordinary, confused human beings driven by needs and circumstances into situations they don't really want to be in, and that we should respond with understanding rather than judgement. The author does not invite a god-like sense of superiority to his characters.

Mr Van Huyten starts taking me over to Leeds and Bradford ... when there's some crack orchestra playing Vic's willingness to learn, to have his horizons broadened, is again shown.

Mussorgsky Russian composer (1835–81).

Tchaikovsky Russian composer (1840–93). The 'old bint' with whom he corresponded but whom he never met was his patroness, the wealthy Madame von Meck. Tchaikovsky died after contracting cholera, caused by drinking unfiltered water. Vic responds, naturally enough, to the glamorous or tragic circumstances of these composers' lives.

Elgar English composer (1857–1934).

It's crap, but if she likes it it's her dough The reaction illustrates not only the gap between Vic's tastes and Ingrid's, but also the dismissive, even contemptuous way he regards her.

I don't suppose she means a bint I've never yet laid eyes on, that exists only in my mind No rival exists to Ingrid, except in Vic's imagination, which can conjure up a picture of his ideal partner much more potent than reality can provide.

And as for all this – she started it, didn't she? The tone – both aggressive and defensive – reflects the thinker's discomfort. He is being forced into a corner, to define the exact nature of his feelings for Ingrid, and the alternative explanations she offers are equally uncomfortable (either he loved her or he wanted her only for sex). Vic retaliates by trying to blame her.

I start paying my board at home A sign that Vic has passed into adulthood. He can no longer be financially dependent on his parents.

She's got all sorts of little ways that put me on edge. Compare this with almost any statement he makes about her in the early part of the novel. Then everything delighted him.

Me, I like to look English because I reckon it's the finest country in the world, bar none The simple patriotism is characteristic of the narrator, but the upbeat quality of the remark is balanced by the (equally characteristic) sympathy he expresses for the tramp sitting in the café – 'you can't help feeling sorry and kind of sick inside to look at him'.

Chapter 4

This key chapter carries the couple's relationship past the point of no return. Ingrid's pregnancy fastens each to the other. What happens here is hardly unusual, either in reality or in fiction (another important novel of the time, *Saturday Night and Sunday Morning*, also describes an unwanted pregnancy), and Vic himself is well aware that his predicament isn't new; among the painful mixture of feelings is the consciousness of being a fool, as he imagines all the 'blokes (who) must have been in this pickle' laughing at 'another poor sod' added to the long line 'stretching right back to ancient times'. But, of course, however common the situation, it is – or was – no less disastrous for the individual; and Vic is consumed with fear, anger at himself and self-pity. Sympathy with Ingrid only comes later. Although the narrator's almost exclusive concern with himself may not be a particularly attractive feature of his character – there are moments when the reader may want to say, 'What about *her*?' – it is consistent with the honesty and candour of his presentation in the novel. Barstow does not shy away from a direct portrayal of sexual desire, but without falling into the insistent explicitness of more recent writing, nor does he try to conceal the less appealing aspects of his central character. Vic can be selfish, bitter, crude and so on. In a panic he thinks of himself and feels towards Ingrid only an intense regret at having met her in the first place.

The present-day reader of *A Kind of Loving* may have to make an imaginative effort to sympathize with Vic and Ingrid's predicament. For Barstow is writing of a period (just) before the more relaxed moral outlook of the 1960s and after. We see in this chapter that contraception is the responsibility of the male, and that Vic is too timid to do anything about it; that the only response to a pregnancy was a rapid marriage; and that divorce, though feasible, is almost out of the question in the community where Vic lives. Attitudes towards pregnancy, marriage and divorce have changed very considerably over the last thirty years, but it would be wrong to assume that the climate of moral opinion has changed so completely that the responses exhibited by Vic and Ingrid — panic, fear (particularly of what their parents are going to say), shame and humiliation, a sense of having been trapped (on Vic's part) — would not be echoed by those caught in a similar situation today. In any case Barstow's re-creation of the minute oscillations in Vic's mood, the tangle of his emotions, the movement from erotic excitement at the start of the chapter (when the couple are in Ingrid's house) to bitter resignation at the end — all this is rendered so vividly and immediately by the author that the reader's first reaction is not to consider how different the moral climate is *now* but to identify with the characters' troubles *then*.

when they have kids and how many is their business and nobody else's The statement (about Vic's sister and brother-in-law) stands in ironic contrast to the fact that Ingrid's pregnancy, when it becomes known, will be a crisis: their two families will make it very much their business.

if you can look as happy as Chris and David do after a year of it Vic continues to see his sister's marriage as the ideal. Now he considers Ingrid to have been no more than 'a passing fancy'.

it's not as if we were ... well, courting, is it? The remark reflects what Vic's mother has said in the previous section. To be 'courting' in this context is to be involved in a serious relationship that will lead to marriage.

we couldn't tell anybody how it is, could we? Because the relationship has no status, is almost entirely physical, hasn't got the formality of courtship which would oblige them to tell their parents.

I'm not liking this. We've managed pretty well without talk before Vic is made uncomfortable when asked to define his feelings. Although glad to be given the opportunity to 'make some excuse for myself', he is too scrupulous to be able to lie.

'Aye, in your flipping imagination, Willy, I know.' There is more talk about sex than actual activity. Vic sees through his friend.

To get really free, though, I have to get right away from her This paragraph, in which Vic analyses his attitude and behaviour with Ingrid, presents an unhappy, oppressive picture of their times together. Being tied to her, to his own urges and the subsequent twinges of guilt (so that he feels 'just about the rottenest devil alive'), is comparable to being imprisoned. He is momentarily 'released' but never really free. There is 'another way' but it would only occur with the girl that Vic had always dreamed of (see end of paragraph).

But not where I live In Vic's community divorce is rare; in any case it goes against the grain of his instinctive belief that marriage is for life.

'She made me have a hot bath and drink some gin' As a way of getting rid of the baby (a similar episode occurs in *Saturday Night and Sunday Morning*).

'. . . it's a kind of murder, in a way, that . . .' Vic is less hard-headed than Ingrid.

I'm not the only one to have gone through it this past few days. The first touch of sympathy. Ingrid's shame will be greater. But the moment soon passes when he considers that she has at least got what she wanted, himself, while he has nothing.

And a bloody fine catch I am. The thought is, of course, ironic – his self-esteem is at a very low point.

caught . . . trapped Not just by circumstances, but by the girl. The choice of words reveals his hostility towards her, as if she had deliberately set out to trick him.

'I'm no bloody angel but I'm not that kind of louse.' A kind of grudging decency is shown. Vic will do the 'right thing', as would be expected by Ingrid, parents, their society – and not least by himself.

Even if she won't force me, what about everybody else? He is aware of the pressure that will be applied. Only a 'better man' – or a worse one? – could resist it. And we have seen throughout the novel that Vic is an individual with a strong sense of duty and obligation towards others, particularly those of the older generation (his parents, Mr Van Huyten).

Questions and assignments on Chapters 1–4

1 Explain what Vic learns from Conroy and Mr Van Huyten in these chapters. What does this tell us about his character?

2 To what extent do you sympathize with the central character in this part of the novel? Give reasons for your views.

Assignments

1 Imagine that you were the age of Vic or Ingrid in the late 1950s. Looking back from the vantage-point of the present day, write an account of the changes in moral attitudes which you have noted between then and now. Don't assume that everything is automatically better – or worse! – today, but attempt to come to balanced conclusions about, for example, alterations in the general attitude towards marriage (Vic believes it is not something to get out of, but present-day views are less fixed). Alternatively, this exercise could be attempted as a dialogue between two members of a group, one playing the older part. Or you could record a conversation with someone who really was of that generation!

2 Write down some of the diary entries which Ingrid might make, commenting on some of the incidents in this section of the novel. Re-read carefully what she says in these chapters in order to assess what her feelings might be.

Chapter 5

This chapter details the painful embarrassment of Vic's telling his parents about Ingrid and himself and the greater discomfort of having to confront *her* parents. In both cases the fathers are relatively understanding, to the extent that Vic finds himself liking Mr Rothwell, and being surprised at the tolerance shown by his own father. The mothers, however, are suspicious and resentful. Mrs Brown thinks that her son has been trapped by 'some little slut 'at's got her claws into you', although she softens her opinion after meeting Ingrid, declaring her 'a decent enough lass'. Mrs Rothwell is snobbish and sharp-tongued. Vic is alarmed by the prospect, the only one open to the couple, of having to live in her house. Events have passed out of his control. His only feelings are an overwhelming helplessness and a desperate desire that things should be restored to how they were.

'An' if our Victor's had his fun he's a right to pay for it just like anybody else.' The Old Feller's direct and simple morality is not vindictive but an expression of his instinctive sense that enjoyment must be paid for, that adult responsibilities have to be assumed.

'We don't want 'em thinkin' you come from any sort of family.' Not a snobbish attitude, unlike Mrs Rothwell's, but an attempt to uphold the dignity and good name of the family – something that is very much the preserve of the mother.

Ingrid goes out and doesn't come straight back. The scene has obviously been prearranged. It is Mr Rothwell's job to find out about Vic, especially his career prospects.

'Women are always a lot more emotional about these things.' Mr Rothwell wins Vic over partly by his calm and friendly manner, partly by this kind of appeal to a shared male outlook.

I can feel it all closing in round me like a big net. The arrival of Mrs Rothwell alarms Vic; she is so evidently hostile.

'We have very good connexions and we've always had high hopes of the match she might make.' The remark is discouragingly snobbish, but this episode might be less plausible if every participant was tolerant and understanding. Antagonism between Vic and his future mother-in-law is established early on.

The kid, though ... I've never really stopped to think about it before. Too preoccupied with the present to consider what's to come, Vic spares only a moment to think of the child. Notice that Barstow does not allow for any sentimentality in Vic's response – he is in no way reconciled to the future.

'we shall just have to make the best of it' This could stand as a comment on the relationship between Vic and Ingrid for the rest of the novel, although the words are actually spoken by her father.

'the nice white wedding I've always imagined Ingrid having' There will be no respectable celebration, as there was at the beginning of the novel. Mrs Rothwell's indignation is in part understandable.

'He could ha' done worse' Vic is pleased with what is actually a piece of 'high praise' from his mother for Ingrid. The scene in which she meets his parents is not described. There have already been enough moments of confrontation and explanation in the chapter.

All my mates ... I'm avoiding like the plague Vic is ashamed of being shown up for a fool because he has been 'trapped'.

Chapter 6

The early days of the marriage are relentlessly chronicled in this chapter. All Vic's feelings from before the wedding – anger, resentment, frustration, helplessness – survive after it. They are even intensified because he now knows he's in a prison from which there is no escape. 'I'm a goner'; 'these casual remarks about us spending the rest of our lives together' terrify him; repeatedly he voices (but only inwardly, of course) his sense of desperation. In a mood to find fault, he objects to Ingrid's snobbish affectations in the hotel where they spend their honeymoon. He comes to see daughter and mother as being somehow in league against him, determined to deny him any residual pleasures (going to a concert or out for a drink). He hates their tastes, their prissiness, their limitations. The mood is exclusively negative and bitter. This is an extremely one-sided account, from the point of view of an intensely disappointed and miserable young man caught up in a situation in which he finds himself having less and less control over the circumstances of his own life. It's irrelevant to criticize the narrative for its partisan or lop-sided quality. Vic – or Barstow – is saying simply, 'This is how it is'. If the central character could project himself imaginatively into the mind and heart of his new wife, could see things from her angle (or even from his mother-in-law's!), then he would be a different kind of person, the narrative would take another course. But to be sympathetic or to identify with somebody else requires, if only for a moment, that you put yourself second, and Vic's outrage and depression are so strong that he has no room to consider the position of those around him.

Now I see she's smiling at me and I feel tons better just for that. The approval – or non-condemnation – of his sister is vital to Vic. He values her opinion above that of anybody else.

I'll be ... wondering if everybody knows, and us on our honeymoon He is as susceptible as the older generation to the shame of their being newly married when Ingrid is obviously pregnant.

knocking-shop Brothel.

'it strikes me you're the snob – an upside-down snob' Ingrid accuses Vic of being so concerned to project a down-to-earth image of himself, unwilling because of a misplaced pride to adjust his manners whatever the circumstances, that his refusal to 'put on airs' becomes in itself a kind of affectation, an inverted snobbery. As he acknowledges to himself, he is 'partly at fault'.

It's not having a life of my own any more that really gets me down Vic can no longer do as he wants; nor do he and Ingrid have any privacy in her parents' house.

This is the way we always are now. The statement – flat, terse – is a depressing measure of how low the couple's relationship has sunk.

'There's no bloody p'raps about it.' Driven by anger and frustration Vic finally gives vent to his regret that they ever married.

Chapter 7

This chapter of accidents moves from disaster to farce. Ingrid's pregnancy ends in a miscarriage. Shaken by the news, and by the fact that his mother-in-law has left him to find out what happened by himself, Vic cannot help seeing the loss of the baby (itself no more to him than 'an egg growing in Ingrid') as a dissolving of the remaining bond between his wife and him. Some surviving sense of obligation towards her, however, stops him from walking away, because 'I think what a rough time Ingrid's had and I can't add to her troubles'. But the reason for their marrying has, ironically, gone now that they are married.

Vic's relationship with his mother-in-law poisons what little feeling remains for Ingrid: he sees the mother in the daughter, her outlook, her manner, even her looks. He is sexually frustrated and bitterly reflects on the opportunities lost to him since, even if he happened to see the right girl now, it would be too late, he is 'a marked man'. Events reach a comic and crude climax when, after a pub crawl with an affluent old school friend (and a minor accident in the latter's car), he returns home to a drunken confrontation with Mrs Rothwell. Vic is boorish and uncontrolled; he is sick on the front-room carpet, is denied Ingrid (who has retreated to her mother's bedroom), and finally falls into a drunken sleep. The chapter finishes with his sneaking from his wife's home, intending presumably to put it and her behind him for good.

It is hard to say where the balance of sympathy lies as the marriage reaches a point where it appears to have broken beyond repair. Is Vic the victim, goaded beyond endurance by the oppressive rule of Mrs Rothwell and what he sees as a kind of conspiracy between her and her daughter? Certainly there is some provocation for his actions, and the behaviour of mother (and sometimes, daughter) does suggest that she is attempting either to mould Vic or to exclude him altogether from her and Ingrid's lives. Both penned in and pushed out (because he is not admitted as a properly legitimate member of his wife's family), Vic responds with fits of frustration and anger. In such situations, however, right can very rarely be on one side only. Barstow shows how in this triangular relationship – triangular because Mrs Rothwell is 'competing' with Vic for Ingrid, and the man is by no means sure that he wants her anyway – spite and dislike are piled one on top of another. None of the three is able to get out of this spiral of hostility, and Vic's 'escape' at the end is more apparent than real.

I haven't a key Suggests how little Vic is trusted or accepted in the Rothwell household. He still has the status of unwelcome visitor.

I know it and so do Mr and Mrs Oliphant. Vic knows that Mrs Rothwell could have contacted him with the bad news. Mrs Oliphant contrives a face-saving formula, but the knowledge is humiliating as well as profoundly hurtful to him.

What if I'm a widower just this minute and I don't know it? Free again ... Callous, possibly, but this is a speculation rather than a wish, and one not unnaturally thrown up in the turmoil of his response. It shows how alienated he is from Ingrid.

They're nice people. Nice and steady and quiet and happy ... All the things that he and Ingrid are not. He sees everybody's life as preferable to his own.

Sex without complications, and love could wait till the right girl came along Vic's attitude has simplified since the beginning of the novel.

tash Moustache.

This is what it all comes to, is it? ... I never wanted much in the first place, just a girl I could love ... one I could be pals with The tone is self-pitying. Vic has reached the lowest point in his view of himself and his relationships. At the same time his sorrow for himself is qualified by an awareness that he is responsible for what has occurred.

Chapter 8

Vic walks out but soon discovers that he cannot walk away from what he has made of his life. His sister, kindly but firmly, brings him face to face with his responsibilities; his mother refuses to see him until he has repaired the damage done; and he is compelled to face Ingrid's father. A combination of factors – failure to get the kind of support he expected from his family, the offer of a flat for Ingrid and himself, Mr Rothwell's calm and persuasive analysis of Vic's predicament, and his willingness to listen to his son-in-law's side of the argument – all these together press Vic to approach his wife once more, to attempt to put their relationship on a new footing. Vic can be advised by his sister and father-in-law, and will listen to the advice because he respects the speakers, but ultimately the choices and decisions are his own. He is free to go back into the marriage – or not. It is the first truly adult decision he has to make.

'You say that?' He is appalled because if his sister is critical of him then he cannot expect understanding from any quarter.

'Trust Chris to get me out of it ... It's a bit too big for that.' Vic's sister tells him that there is no magic solution which she can deliver. He must abandon the childish reflex of running to someone older in the hope that she can rescue him. Vic has already had a premature adulthood thrust on him, in the shape of the unwanted marriage and pregnancy; now he is being eased into an emotional maturity.

It's the worst of being here, seeing how happy they are. In the ideal partnership, which he has failed to achieve.

'all romance and rapture and starry eyes' A good description of the early stages of his affair with Ingrid. Chris's point – and it is not an easy one to make without lapsing into either sentimentality or sermonizing – is that the excitement of being 'in love' (which, in Vic's case, depended heavily on his not really knowing what Ingrid was like), is different from 'loving' as a result of shared experience, a life constructed together. It is this joint existence which the couple have not allowed themselves to build yet.

'Losing the baby was more of an ordeal to her than it could be to you.' An obvious statement, perhaps, though not one Vic would have articulated for himself.

'Why did you get married? ... Because you loved Ingrid or because of the baby?' The question indicates Mr Rothwell's shrewdness. Vic is made uncomfortable and takes refuge in silence, but the other's good-humoured response shows that he is not eager to condemn his son-in-law. For Vic his marriage has been bitter precisely because he didn't love Ingrid, yet had to keep up in front of their families the pretence that he did, both to save face and to redeem his behaviour.

Chapter 9

The end of *A Kind of Loving* is not a real conclusion. It is a re-beginning of Vic's and Ingrid's marriage, on a surer footing but with no certainty as to its ultimate success. The end is provisional rather than final, and it is towards this uncertain, midly hopeful point that the book has been directed. Indeed, it is implicit in its very title. Vic has not achieved the absolute relationship with the woman of his dreams (the cliché may be appropriate when we think of his earlier visions of the idealized 'right girl'). Instead he has to settle in an ungrudging and mature fashion for an intimacy that is less than perfect – a *kind* of loving. His optimism is tempered by experience. He has accommodated himself to reality, is at last at ease with himself because he is 'doing the right thing'. Instead of kicking against his bad luck and blaming others he assumes – rather than having it forced on him – adult responsibility for the course of his and Ingrid's lives. In this way the novel has chronicled the development of the central character from dependence to self-reliance. He has learned something 'about life and everything' and his conclusions are presented in a typically understated, almost embarrassed manner ('So endeth the lesson.'); but they are no less genuine and deeply felt for being ordinary or conventional in the impression they give of squaring up to life as it is, while retaining a poignant sense of how different things might have been.

You couldn't believe how different she is when her mother's not around. An indication of how his feelings have modified, and of how oppressive he found the circumstances of their early married life.

'my lines' Marriage lines, a certificate of marriage.

So that's all right, then. What is the tone of this inner comment? Ingrid says that she loves Vic but he cannot yet respond. Is he being cynical, wry, expressing satisfaction or resignation? The remark indicates the distance remaining between himself and his wife, and is characteristic of the uncertainty that he is experiencing about the resumption of their relationship.

you've got to do your best and hope for the same A reductive and simple philosophy but one that is appropriate for someone who has had to discard his visions and illusions. It is a hard-won lesson which the novel as a whole endorses.

It's a chilly night and I shiver a bit as I walk. There is no romantic, 'walking into the sunset together' conclusion. The novel ends, two years on, in the same season in which it began.

Questions and assignments on Chapters 5–9

1 Describe the difference in character between Mr and Mrs Rothwell and the impact they make upon Vic.

2 'In the last chapter Vic makes a rapid transition from irresponsibility to maturity.' Comment on this statement.

3 How satisfactory do you find the end of *A Kind of Loving*? Give reasons for your view.

Assignments

1 The central character, and Ingrid, have to face their parents with unwelcome news. Describe an occasion when you have had to tell someone older than yourself something you did not want to say.

2 Dramatize the scene in which Ingrid meets Vic's parents, either in written form or as a group exercise. Base your response on what you have learnt about the characters.

Stan Barstow's art in *A Kind of Loving*
Narrative technique

There are many ways of telling a story, perhaps as many styles, approaches, tones as there are good writers. But a novelist is inevitably limited when he comes to choosing the viewpoint from which his narrative should be delivered. At one extreme is the traditional 'God's eye view' from which the writer supervises the entire action, tells us what is going on in different places, claims the authority of being able to see into the hearts and minds of his characters, and even to know them better than they may know themselves. In this kind of story the writer is aware of everything (as he should be, since the book embodies a world he has himself created), and makes no pretence otherwise. At the opposite extreme is the narrative which is delivered in the first person, from the viewpoint of an individual who is a participant in the action of the novel. This is the case in *A Kind of Loving* where the narrator is also the principal character. The book is the story of two years in the life of Vic Brown, and he tells that story.

First-person narrative

A great advantage of first-person narration is that it invites the reader to share in the teller's life more directly and immediately than any other type of narration. The 'I' who is telling the story communicates without obstruction with 'me', each individual reader. A kind of 'dialogue' is established when the reader responds – as he or she should if the book is working effectively – to the crises, problems, pleasures, etc., of the figure who tells us what he does, thinks, feels. Such first-person narration is the equivalent of the soliloquies in Shakespeare; as when, for example, Hamlet detaches himself from the action on stage and addresses the audience directly, or at least gives us the impression that we are privileged to listen to his most private concerns. We 'overhear' him talking to himself. And in a first-person novel such as *A Kind of Loving* each reader is 'eavesdropping' on the private thoughts and feelings of the narrator. Some of these thoughts may be very private, not to be communicated to anyone. For instance, Vic does not let on to even those closest to him that he does not in fact love Ingrid when he is 'forced' into a marriage with her; and when his sister and father-in-law touch on the subject later he becomes very uneasy. Similarly, when his wife falls downstairs and has a miscarriage, his first response after the initial shock is, 'What if I'm a widower just this minute and I don't know it? Free again ...'. This is not the kind of response he would divulge to anyone; its bluntness and detachment would obviously put him in a very bad light. Why don't we, then, judge him so harshly? The answer probably has to do with the kind of bond that is forged between reader and narrator in *A Kind of Loving*.

Most people are gratified to be given confidences by someone, to be told secrets, to be allowed a glimpse into another's inner life. Apart from the intrinsic interest of what one may be told, there is the pleasure that can come from having earned the trust of the other person. Conversely, most of us are careful whom we give our confidences to, for obvious reasons. Where a confidence or secret is given, then an understanding or complicity is created between the two individuals concerned. Something of this applies to the link between teller and listener/reader in a story where the narrator unfolds his life – in all its aspects, working, social, sexual and so on – without apparently holding anything back. The sense of 'privilege' this bestows on the reader, because he is, as it were, inside the narrator's head and knows him better than any character in the novel, is one of the most powerful reasons for relating a story in the first person. Unless the speaker is extremely unsympathetic we are, almost automatically, biased in his favour because he is telling us things he would never tell anyone else. We are in on all the 'secrets'.

It should be noted, in passing, that there is a temptation in reading a novel like *A Kind of Loving* (first-person narrative, realistic in its treatment of daily life) to assume that the storyteller is the same as the author. In fact, *the narrator is as much of an invention as any of the other characters;* he is not to be confused with the real-life author who made him up. We should not, therefore, jump to the conclusion that the author endorses or 'approves of' everything that the 'I' does in the course of the action. There are examples of classic novels (*Great Expectations, Huckleberry Finn*) where, despite the fundamental sympathy we have with the narrators, there is a considerable gap between the teller and the real author, and we are intended to see that the narrators are, in various ways, at fault, imperceptive, foolish, etc. So the fact that a novel is written in the first person, and an appeal made thereby for our understanding and sympathy, does not preclude our judging and assessing the character talking to us.

A Kind of Loving is written *entirely in the present tense*. Most fiction is written in the past tense; that is, what is set down on the page has already occurred. In Barstow's novel, what we read is set down as it is happening, or so it seems. This stylistic choice – past or present tense; things *having happened* before they are described or things apparently *happening now* as you read the words – is not an insignificant one. Like the decision to use a first-person narrator, the choice of the continuous present adds to the immediacy and impact of the novel. The reader is offered the illusion that what is unfolding on the page is not safely over and done with, tucked up in the past, but taking place now in the (possibly) dangerous or exciting present moment – 'dangerous' or 'exciting' because we don't know where the present might lead, whereas we already know what the past has led us to. In addition, the use of the continuous present in *A Kind of Loving* reflects the way all of us respond to the world in the inner commentary we provide for ourselves in our heads as we encounter one thing after another. The 'stream of consciousness' technique which Barstow employs in his central character – a technique in which thoughts, feelings, observations, memories, and so on, are placed before the reader in an almost random fashion to reproduce the haphazard way we respond to the jumble of life – such a stream of consciousness is expressed most appropriately in the present tense, since our consciousness must inevitably be most preoccupied with the here-and-now. If you open almost any page of *A Kind of Loving* you will receive the impression that the narrator is 'merely' recording (in documentary style) what he sees, what he does, what happens to him, *as it occurs*.

The book thus gives off a random, accidental air – it is 'like life'. Minor characters are introduced without much explanation, meetings and conversations take place which seem to have no great significance, events are not neatly rounded off at the end of the story. This air of randomness is fitting. It is an 'accident' or 'slip up' (Ingrid's getting pregnant) that precipitates the crisis in the novel. And one of the conclusions that Vic reaches at the end is that 'no secret, and no God and no heaven and no hell' exist. There is no plan to things. They 'just' happen. The content and the narrative style of the novel continually reinforce this point.

One final aspect should be mentioned. The *diction*, or *choice of language* made by the author is naturally a reflection of the personality and 'position' of his narrator. It has to be, otherwise we would find it difficult to believe in Vic Brown. The narrative style is relaxed, informal, colloquial, sometimes making use of slang or dialect. One example will do: from the episode where Vic and his father go to the former's old school:

Me and the Old Man tag on to the line. I'm easy about giving blood now; it's a doddle; but I can never get used to the hospital smell they bring with them when they come and set up for the job. The Old Feller goes in and I follow in half a minute and sit down in front of this bod who takes my card. (Chapter 6, Part One)

The style is casual. Colloquial in its syntax ('Me and the Old Man') and in the terms used ('doddle', 'bod'), it suggests – so persuasively and realistically that by this stage in the novel we've long stopped thinking about it or even being aware of it – that we are listening to someone carelessly 'recording' his impromptu thoughts and reactions, more for his own benefit than anyone else's. Above all, such a style sounds 'real' or 'natural'. It is, of course, a literary feat, as hard to achieve – perhaps harder – than the most artificial piece of prose. Barstow's style in *A Kind of Loving* is conversational, flexible, unpretentious, and, most important, clear. You don't have to go back and read a bit of the story twice because you are unsure of its meaning. If such clarity and ease seem to you straightforward to accomplish, then try to imitate them, describing an everyday event in simple, readable, everyday English!

In summary, the narrative of *A Kind of Loving* depends for its effect on its first-person point of view and on the use of a fluent, confiding, colloquial style appropriate to the principal character. The factors that have been separated for the purposes of comment in this section actually work together on the page. We cannot detach the manner of telling the story from the storyteller; indeed, the way in which he 'talks' is vital to our understanding of his personality.

Characters

Vic Brown

I'm like thousands of others

The narrator and central character, Vic provides the eyes
through which we witness the action of the entire novel. We are
therefore influenced not only by what he sees but by the way that
he sees it. As a character he is all-important.

Barstow never presents Vic as someone out of the ordinary.
His aspirations and hopes, fears and consolations are in no sense
unconventional. 'I'm like thousands of others,' he says of his
feeling of unease at going into a hospital (trying to visit Ingrid
after her miscarriage), and the remark is applicable to almost
every aspect of his life. He is modest in his assessment of himself: 'as presentable as the next bloke', but in his view less
intelligent than his brother and sister; ready to change jobs but
out of restlessness rather than ambition. He is something of a
conformist (look at the scene where their employer, Althorpe, is
rebuking Vic and Conroy for fighting in the office) and does not
adopt the rebellious or resentful stance of other 'heroes' of
novels set in this period. He respects his parents, even if he
sometimes gets a bit impatient with them. He has a high regard
for the rest of his family. He works uncomplainingly, and brings
a real enthusiasm to the task of reorganizing the record shop.
Vic's way of life and his outlook, like those of his family, are
essentially decent and respectable. He isn't attracted by the
'mucky ways' of his friend Willy's mother and her family's
squalid and casual style (see Chapter 4, section III, in Part Two).
When he disgraces himself by being sick in front of Mrs Rothwell and then by 'bawling and swearing' he compares his
behaviour to that of 'people in a slum'. Compelled to do the
'right thing' in marrying Ingrid after her pregnancy is discovered, he does not rebel, but after a period of intolerable
frustration and self-pity, he *chooses* to do the 'right thing' *for
himself* by returning to her voluntarily.

Vic Brown acts in this manner not because he is too feeble to
stand up to others or because he has an excessive desire to

please. He respects only those who merit respect (compare the different attitudes he shows towards Althorpe and Hassop, in the Drawing Office). There is much affection and admiration in his feelings for his parents, mingled (in relation to his mother at least) with a touch of fearfulness. This testifies to the secure niche he occupies in the rigid structure of this working-class family. The portrait that Barstow is painting in *A Kind of Loving* – or self-portrait, if one thinks of the book as having been 'written' by Vic – is of a man who is tolerant, decent, warm-hearted, often confused and uncertain of himself, conscientious, and sensitive to a degree he wouldn't acknowledge openly. His personality is more complex than it appears, or than he lets it appear, on the surface.

Vic keeps his vulnerable side well hidden. When in company with his friends he is 'one of the lads', on the edge of the jokes and the sexual innuendo. He can't afford to seem different – though in many ways, of course, he is the same as his friends – because he is aware that, were he to tell them of the ideal girl who exists so far only in his imagination, they would call him 'sloppy and soft in the head'. His hopes or vision for marriage and partnership extend a long way beyond the limited sexual ambitions espoused by the young male community he associates with. His search is for 'the other person who will make (him) whole', as his sister defines it. Vic would never put it so clearly; he would not risk the overtone of pretension in the remark. Nevertheless, this is the object of his search or, at least, remains his imaginative ideal. The more entangled and sexually involved Vic becomes with Ingrid the more he sees that she nowhere comes near his 'ideal'. He can't, however, summon up the nerve to break things off – he is anyway getting some enjoyment (as well as a fair dose of guilt) out of the sexual side of their relationship – and, victim to a combination of cowardice, obligation and pleasurable inertia, he eventually finds himself sentenced to a prison of a marriage ('The cell door shuts behind me') with a woman he'd never considered as a life-long partner since their first couple of outings together. By the end of *A Kind of Loving* he has developed or matured enough to accept his share in the failure of a marriage that had hardly got under way. He expresses the desire to start again. Perhaps such development also entails his discarding, at any rate for the moment, his (immature?) vision of the ideal partner.

Vic Brown therefore fulfils what is possibly the principal demand made by the reader on the central figure in a piece of fiction. He changes, is not the same at the end of the book as he was in the beginning. Such development may not always be for the better (one could say, in the cliché, that Vic is 'sadder but wiser' in the end) but it is the process of alteration itself which engages the reader and gives the impression that the novel is faithfully reflecting the changes (the alterations in perspective, the different way we look at things as we grow older) that are inseparable from living.

Vic is an attractive character. He has to be, if we're to remain listening to him for the length of the book. There are moments when we may consider him boorish, insensitive, veering towards dishonesty (hardly major faults), but throughout we retain an interest in his narrative, a sympathy for his predicaments, and often an identification with his outlook.

Ingrid

a decent enough lass

As a character Ingrid exists, like all the other figures in the novel, only as she is seen through Vic's eyes. Vic is not an impartial observer of Ingrid. At the start he regards her as an unattainable goddess. At a low point near the end she reminds Vic of the mother-in-law he detests. She is the same character but Vic's feelings about her have swung from one extreme to the other.

She is a typist at the engineering firm where Vic works as a draughtsman. It is significant that she is described not in the detached and fairly detailed manner that Vic brings to bear on some of the minor characters (e.g. his description of Henry or of Hassop's sister) but in rather vague terms that tell us more about Vic's response than they do about Ingrid's appearance: she is 'trim', 'smart', 'a smashing piece'. He is too much in love with her to see her clearly. Later on he is so out of love that he cannot appreciate her at all, except physically.

There are early hints that her tastes are different from Vic's – an unimportant gap at the time but it will matter in the future. In addition, her distaste for reading and fondness for 'telly' suggest she hasn't got the curiosity or desire to extend herself that Vic possesses. In his prejudiced view, what she likes in music is 'crap', while he refuses to concede that she's ever had 'a serious thought to call her own'. He sees her as affected, snobbish, mean-spirited (for example, in the quarrel over his giving money to a tramp). She is certainly conventional in her outlook and expectations – but the same could be said of Vic.

Ingrid is perceptive enough in her analysis of their uneasy relationship, sufficiently so to cause Vic some embarrassment when they are alone in her parents' house. There is no doubt that she loves Vic and wishes to marry him. When their situation improves at the end of the novel, she shows a greater confidence in the future and is more than willing to re-start the marriage. Vic warms to her once more, and attributes his more affectionate attitude towards his wife to the fact that his mother-in-law isn't there!

It has to be said that Ingrid doesn't emerge as a character in her own right in *A Kind of Loving*. Not that she is implausible – as with all the figures in the novel, she is rendered with Barstow's naturalistic touch so as to be instantly convincing. It is rather that she never comes out from under the shadow of Vic's strong feelings (love or near hate) about her. She says little, and when she does speak – as, for example, to voice her fear that Vic will think her 'common' because she has given way to him physically – what she says is exactly what one might expect of any girl of her age, class, outlook, upbringing, time. She suffers more than Vic does, she has to endure the pregnancy and the miscarriage, but her suffering is made marginal, or somehow partly redeemed by her having got what she wanted (Vic as husband) while he has achieved nothing. It is left to another, more articulate woman character (Vic's sister, Chris) to point out that she has been through an 'ordeal' and now needs 'somebody strong'. But this male narrative does not allow much breathing-space for a woman's point of view.

Vic's parents: Mr and Mrs Brown

The Old Man; the Old Lady. The terms show the easy, affectionate way in which Vic regards his father and mother. His father is a pit deputy and still slightly surprised to be earning, at last, a 'decent livin' wage' for his labour. He can remember harder times but, unlike some of the other older characters, he does not appear to look at the present in an apprehensive spirit, afraid that another slump is inevitable. Mr Brown is proud of his children, places a high value on education (it is one of the reasons he respects his new son-in-law, David), and is gratified by his children's achievements. Vic is a little taken aback to discover this – 'it's never occurred to me he might be proud of me'. The comment is simultaneously an index of Vic's modesty and of his father's unenvious satisfaction in the fact that his children have opportunities never available to him. He does not have a large part to play in the novel but Barstow stresses his capacity to reconcile: his speech at the wedding of Chris and David is full of praise for family harmony; his intervention when Vic has revealed the news of Ingrid's pregnancy is on the side of tolerance and understanding. He represents an older working-class tradition of life-time service to one occupation and uncomplaining acceptance of a sometimes laborious or harsh existence, lightened by diversions such as playing the trombone ('He's had offers from some tip-top bands in his time'), or following the progress of his children.

The 'Old Lady' is an altogether more formidable figure. She too is in a working-class tradition. She is the linchpin of the household, supervisor of her husband and children's lives, their health and bed-times, their careers and prospects. Like her husband, she takes a pride in the children but can also be something of a domestic tyrant. Vic is a little frightened by her. She occasionally reminds him that he's not too big 'for a good slap', a threat he takes seriously. Her maternal advice and queries are well meant but Vic finds them faintly oppressive, especially when she starts to ask questions about his relationship with Ingrid. As the upholder of the family dignity and good name, she is more hurt than her husband by the revelation that Vic is marrying. She is concerned that her prospective daughter-in-law's family should get the right impression of *her* family. 'All she thinks of is position and income and character' says Vic, remarking on her attitude towards the marriage of Chris and David, and although Mrs Brown does not indulge in snobbery for its own sake she does place a high value on the things Vic lists. Underneath the rather crusty exterior – a manner abrasive, inquisitive, sometimes interfering – there is a fund of common sense, usually expressed in proverbial terms, and a genuine warm-heartedness.

Ingrid's parents: Mr and Mrs Rothwell

Although not introduced into the novel until its closing stages, they are significant figures because their words and actions give shape to Vic and Ingrid's marriage. Mr Rothwell is a calm, conciliatory man (like Vic's own father). Vic pays tribute to him in the final chapter, and indeed it is he who is largely responsible for bringing the couple together again. He summons Vic to an interview but, instead of rebuking his son-in-law, he listens to his grievances and shrewdly penetrates to the heart of Vic's feelings. He allows the younger man his say and then, rationally and gently, urges him towards a position from where he can resume married life without loss of self-respect. He appeals to the better side of Vic's nature, gives him confidence in himself by declaring his own confidence ('I don't shy from the thought of you being my son-in-law'). Vic has been impressed with him from their first meeting; his friendliness and practicality take away something of the profound embarrassment and shame he feels.

By contrast, Mrs Rothwell is spiteful and hostile. Her physical appearance indicates severity or disapproval – 'pressed tight', 'well corseted', 'little mouth all pursed up' – and she immediately signals her antagonism towards Vic. In part this is based on an understandable anger over what has happened to her daughter, but this is expressed in such a snobbish fashion that the reader's potential sympathy is withdrawn. When Vic and Ingrid move into her parents' home after the wedding, Mrs Rothwell joins battle with her son-in-law for possession of the daughter. She wants to get Ingrid on her side, to take her back. There are disputes over music, television, drinking and so on. There is a crisis when Mrs Rothwell deliberately fails to inform Vic that his wife has had a bad accident and is in hospital. There is another crisis when Vic returns home drunk, and all the bad feeling between him and Mrs Rothwell, veiled up till now behind a minimal civility, bursts through. She becomes, for Vic, a hateful, villainous figure. If he is to live with Ingrid again, they must be away from the poisonous influence of her mother. From this summary, it might seem that this character comes near to being a caricature, a crude and exaggerated version of a dragon-like mother-in-law, a familiar enough object for male comedians. In fact, Barstow's characterization is deft and detailed. We find it easy to accept as life-like this portrait of a woman whose petty snobberies and trivial grouses are the outward manifestations of her fury that her daughter has married a 'little upstart'.

Other characters

There are many other characters in *A Kind of Loving*. Some of them are discussed in the individual chapter commentaries. They range from the significant – like Chris, Vic's sister, whom he loves and idealizes – to the minor (a girl in the office, an old man in the pub). Some appear only once or twice, or have no discernible function in the novel; they seem to have just 'wandered in'. This treatment of characters, their often casual appearance or disappearance from the action, is intentional. It reinforces one of the strongest features of the novel, its surface realism. As in life, people 'turn up' or 'vanish' from view without necessarily having to account for their movements. Those who matter to Vic stay in the centre of his vision. The rest flicker in the corner of his eye, glimpsed and then forgotten. It is another aspect of the illusion Barstow brings off in *A Kind of Loving*: that we are listening not to something that is made up but to something that really happened.

Joby
Introduction

Joby is a tolerant and generous book. It is truthful and touching,
but never sentimental in its evocation of what life was like for
one ordinary boy in a Yorkshire town in the couple of months
that preceded the outbreak of the Second World War. The book
doesn't look back on a nostalgically golden age, or pretend that
these are the happiest days of Joby's life.

As indicated in the individual chapter commentaries, Barstow
presents the child's world as something that coincides only in
part with the adult one. Children inhabit a slightly different
territory – emotional, intellectual, social – to that lived in by
grown-ups. Their dreams and fears may be sharper, more
absorbing than the adult equivalents. Barstow does not go as far
as other novelists who have dealt with childhood – for example,
Richard Hughes in *A High Wind in Jamaica* (1929) or William
Golding in *Lord of the Flies* (1954) – and offer a vision of children
as strange or disturbing beings who might almost have come
from another planet. But he does acknowledge that to be a child
is to be pleased, frightened, consoled, anxious, in ways that
sometimes disappear with the arrival of maturity.

It is part of this transitional, growing-up stage – difficult and
uncomfortable, interesting and inescapable – that Stan Barstow
is concerned with in *Joby*. The central character is changing, in
his emotions and his understanding, and there is change all
around him. Mrs Weston's departure for hospital loosens the
family ties; Joby's father's relationship with his niece Mona provokes a crisis; Joby himself is between schools, and might also be
said to be 'between' friends, as he shifts his loyalties in the course
of the narrative. And, as a background to all this, there is the
larger historical change that occurred at the end of the 1930s
culminating in the outbreak of World War II in September,
1939 (the novel finishes before this point).

What then are the components of Joby's world, its pleasures
and terrors? There is a good deal of fear and anxiety, obviously.
Joby spends much time in a state of apprehension: will his
mother be safe in hospital? When is his father going to return?
Will he get into trouble because of the shoplifting? and so on.

Some of these fears are well-founded. Others, such as his anxieties over Elsa or Mollie, have their humorous aspect. The thread of disaster, imminent or actual, runs through the novel. Death and abandonment are always possible. There is a suicide (of Snap's uncle) which makes Joby fear for his own father; a reported death of a child (in the letter which Joby cannot read to the old lady); the fact of war (Joby romanticizes the Spanish Civil War in his day dreams, so that it turns into a comic-book story or a Saturday cinema serial, with the goodies always coming out on top). There is the looming presence of the hospital, a 'great repair shop' where people sometimes 'went in and didn't come out'. These things give to the novel a sombre shading, as does the reader's awareness that the crisis in international politics, sparingly referred to only in the first few chapters and of almost no significance to Joby, is leading smoothly and inevitably to September 1939 and the outbreak of World War II.

Barstow does not, however, stress or overplay the darker side of Joby's life. While the novel as a whole could not be described as overtly optimistic (or pessimistic) it does end on a note of what one might term 'realistic hopefulness', when father and son return home together to face their problems. As in *A Kind of Loving* there is the sense that things may work out – at least for a time. This aside, there are other consoling facets of Joby's life. As a child, he is naturally resilient. He has a large store of delights and compensations, including friendship, acceptance by other boys, going to the pictures and reading comics (and *Coral Island*), joining secret societies and day-dreaming. The pleasures may be small or uncomplicated – 'Bought fish and chips and the *Hotspur* made Friday dinner-time one of Joby's favourite times of the week.' – but they are eagerly awaited and intensely experienced. He makes the most of them, just as the whole working-class community makes the most of its seaside holiday week. Joby, or rather his family, is not well-off, certainly not by post-war standards. He wonders whether his parents will be able to afford to buy him a watch to take to the grammar school; he concludes that they probably won't. But, in a more important sense, he does not lead an impoverished life. His childhood satisfactions are only indirectly dependent on money (although Barstow lays proper emphasis on Joby's calculations over his 'Saturday spend'). And the real 'wealth' of Joby's life lies not principally in material pleasures, or in his friendships, but in the consciousness of being accepted and loved by his parents. The process isn't one-way. At the start of the novel Joby loves and relies on his mother and father, in the unthinking manner of the child. By the end, he has moved towards the more difficult, more mature position of seeing them as distinct individuals in need – like him – of love and acceptance.

Joby – chapter commentaries, textual notes, revision questions and assignments

Chapter 1

In little more than a dozen pages the first chapter maps out the reference points in Joby's life: the people that matter most to him, the circumstances that shape his existence. In some ways the day's beginning is typical – Joby meets a schoolfriend, plays with his toy cars. But the morning also has 'something extraordinary' to it, because Joby's mother is going into hospital. Naturally the boy is anxious, the more so when he learns from his parents' unguarded conversation that his mother will be 'cut' in an operation. This event is significant, not only because it frightens Joby on his mother's behalf but because it undermines his implicit belief in the security and reliability offered by the adult world. His mother is vulnerable to illness and, perhaps more important, to fear and anxiety which are suppressed for the sake of the child. This painful realization is one of several moments in the novel when Joby sees that adults are not the stable, unflawed and dependable beings that he had assumed them to be. As he crosses the border from childhood to adolescence he will perceive that the world is often complex and confusing. He begins to lose the straightforward and naïve outlook of the child. In short, he starts to grow up.

he was the boss in Germany The description of Hitler, like that of the German people in the same sentence, accurately reflects a child's limited knowledge of (and interest in) politics. The term 'boss' is one Joby might have heard adults apply to employers; so he uses it to describe someone powerful and 'in charge'. The historical references in the first few paragraphs quickly establish the period as the summer of 1939.

Hitler and Mr Chamberlain and Mussolini Neville Chamberlain (1869–1940) was the British Prime Minister between 1937 and 1940. He was identified with the policy of 'appeasement' towards Hitler whereby it was hoped that the German dictator's ambitions for German expansion would be satisfied by various concessions. The principal concession was the surrender to Germany of a German-speaking area of Czechoslovakia, an agreement made between Chamberlain, Hitler, the Italian dictator Mussolini and the French

Prime Minister at the Munich conference in September 1938. It was after this conference that Chamberlain assured the British people that the agreement had secured 'peace in our time'. In the period leading up to Munich there was a widespread belief that war with Germany was inevitable; hence the instruction which the boys in Joby's school had been given in the use of gas-masks.

Joby is set towards the end of the year of uneasy peace between the Munich treaty and the outbreak of the Second World War. These events serve as a backdrop to what is happening in the novel. Joby isn't much concerned with what is going on in the wider world and most of the adult characters are preoccupied with pressing personal troubles.

Abyssinia The African nation (now Ethiopia) conquered by Italy, under the dictatorship of Mussolini, in 1936.

his uncle's adventures in the Spanish Civil War This sounds at first like another of Snap's inventions but his uncle (a character several times referred to although not actually appearing in the novel) had evidently fought in Spain against the Fascists. The Spanish Civil War lasted from 1936 to 1939. The Republican (government) forces were opposed by the rebels led by General Franco, to whom assistance was given by the Fascist dictatorships of Germany and Italy. The Republicans had support from, among others, an International Brigade – those (like Snap's uncle) drawn to fight the spread of fascism in Europe. References to the Civil War, the Abyssinian campaign and the likelihood of war with Germany indicate the profoundly anxious political climate of the late 1930s.

he wasn't particularly bright at schoolwork Joby admires Snap for his knowledge of out-of-the-way matters and for his inventive imagination. He is not conventionally academic and has failed to get into the grammar school, so Joby will leave his best friend behind in the coming year.

'I don't know why you wouldn't let your Daisy take you down this morning.' The first words spoken by Joby's father immediately establish his grudging, complaining character. He doesn't want to lose a morning's pay and is frightened by the thought of accompanying his wife to the hospital. It's an experience he would rather avoid, and this evasive streak in his nature is confirmed by other incidents in the novel.

'Well you'll meet a lot more boys when you get to the grammar school.' Joby's mother disapproves of Snap as a dreamer and story-teller. She expects her son to associate with more 'suitable' companions at the grammar school.

'That bloomin' 'Itler's at it again,' he said. 'Bletherin' about Poland now.' As part of a plan to restrain Hitler's territorial ambitions, the British Prime Minister Neville Chamberlain had offered to Poland (in March 1939) an assurance that Britain would come to her aid if her independence were threatened. Hitler's forces moved into Poland on September 1st; the British government issued an ultimatum to the

Germans; and the two countries were at war by September 3rd. Mr Weston's comments here reflect the general public feeling that something had to be 'done' about Hilter.

Mr Churchill Winston Churchill (1874–1965) throughout the 1930s warned against Germany's expansionist ambitions and advocated British rearmament. He was the principal figure in the 'anti-appeasement' camp opposed to Chamberlain. Churchill succeeded Chamberlain as Prime Minister (1940–45).

A curious change had come over Joby's father's voice An early indication of his interest in his niece Mona; his sullen, grudging manner disappears.

Mona favoured her father in appearance i.e. she took after her father rather than her mother in looks. The paragraphs describing her and her life history are presented from the novelist's viewpoint rather than Joby's (that is, they contain information or opinions that the child wouldn't have).

the house was as clean and neat as it always was Reflecting Mrs Weston's orderly, house-proud temperament. As long as she is there things are tidy – and not merely in a material sense. When his mother goes into hospital Joby starts to experience a kind of emotional or moral 'untidiness'.

'Nah look, she can have a taxi if she wants one.' Joby's father is shamed into a belated display of generosity because of the presence of his wife's family.

Chapter 2

In the first chapter we saw Joby mostly in relation to the adults in his life. In this second chapter the focus is on his connection with other children. There is a lengthy conversation with his friend Snap and the encounter with Gus Wilson and his gang. Barstow catches finely the elements of these boys' meetings: the teasing and challenging, the hesitations and embarrassments, the aggression and the warmth. The world of the children (or adolescents) overlaps with the adult one, neither separate from nor absolutely identical with it. In some respects the boys echo grown-ups: Snap and Joby confusedly try to make sense of international affairs; Snap teases his friend about the latter's romantic adoration of Elsa, daughter of Jewish refugees from Germany. But the tone, the approach, the understanding displayed by the children are naturally very different from the equivalent adult qualities.

Barstow does not sentimentalize Joby's world. It is not cosy; it contains fear and risk. On the other hand the author does not lay excessive stress on the darker aspects of a child's life. There are distractions and consolations, and the principal one in this chapter is the closeness which Joby feels to Snap.

Here in real life . . . it was all mixed The difficulty of fixing the line between right and wrong (always so clearly delineated in 'the pictures' that Joby sees on Saturdays) grows as the individual does. In this discussion, it's the behaviour of the two sides in the Spanish Civil War that confuses Joby, for neither side seems to have a monopoly of right (or wrong). The problem is a distant one for the boys, even if they have 'a connection with it through Snap's uncle'. The more immediate problems that Joby faces later bring home the difficulties of distinguishing between right and wrong and of judging actions (his own and other people's), as well as showing him the limitations of judgement.

They Eyeties i.e. the Italians (who overran Abyssinia in 1936).

Gary Cooper US film actor (1901–61).

Mae West US film star (1892–1980) famous for the sexual suggestiveness of her performances.

he could see her with him in the tuppenny rush at the pictures on a Saturday afternoon The summit of Joby's infatuated ambition to be with Elsa. She remains a dream to him, inaccessible in reality; details given in the next two paragraphs suggest the social distance between the two.

We could do with a bloke like him in England As well as inspiring fear and hostility, Hitler also evoked admiration from some English people in the 1930s. Such reported comments in *Joby* give a fair spectrum of the political attitudes of the period.

He scrambled up on to the parapet Joby climbs up partly to check on Gus's story about the couple in the field, partly because to not do so would seem a cowardly avoidance of a challenge.

Joby felt his cheeks burn red Joby is embarrassed – Gus's speculations have hit on what he himself thinks is probably the truth about his mother's operation. The subject is an intimate one, and frightening too. His telling Snap is a sign of trust.

Chapter 3

Joby day-dreams, sitting in the barber's chair. What he imagines is funny, to the reader, but not unsympathetically so. The elements of his reverie are drawn from his daily existence and his aspirations: in a skirmish reminiscent of the Spanish Civil War and in the incongruous setting of his school Joby acts out the role of casual hero, to the admiration of Elsa and his headmaster, who praises him as if he'd just hit a good ball in cricket.

He is a comic-book hero, emerging after the siege wounded but victorious and adored. The gentle observation or re-creation of a boy's dreams is set implicitly against the reality. The talk in the barber's is of Hitler's threats to Poland and the possibility of Britain's going to war with Germany. This is not a situation which will be easily or quickly sorted out. It is only in Joby's imagination that the Fascist forces are rapidly driven away by the arrival of 'the relief column, a company of the King's Own Yorkshire Light Infantry'. But in real life rescue will not always arrive at the last moment.

The second part of the chapter also offers an implicit contrast between day-dream and reality. After imagining himself as the heroic idol of Elsa, Joby returns home. He meets Mollie Macleod, only a year older than him but much more knowing and worldly in sexual matters (as the next chapter illustrates). Inside his home Joby discovers a slightly puzzling scene: his cousin Mona coming out of the bedroom where his father is lying, too ill to go to work. Joby notices but does not interpret some tell-tale signs – Mona's slightly flustered state, the unwillingness of both herself and Mr Weston that his 'illness' should be mentioned to Aunt Daisy. The reader makes the interpretation; something that both uncle and niece are embarrassed should be known has occurred. In his innocence and naïvety Joby does not perceive any of this. A world of adult sexuality is hinted at – as it is by the description of the boys drawn to Agnes, Mollie's older sister; they surround her, 'circling round and round on bikes'. Joby's innocence confirms his status as a child but it also stands in contrast to the faintly devious, surreptitious behaviour of some of the adult characters here.

Mr Eden British foreign secretary who opposed Chamberlain over various issues and resigned from his government (in 1938).
like our kid i.e. Like my sister.
'Take a bob for your spend'. In effect, a reward for Joby's agreeing not to say anything about his father's being off work. A bob was a shilling = 5 pence.

Questions and assignments on Chapters 1–3

1 Using quotation and reference describe the characters of Joby's parents as revealed in these opening chapters.

2 List some of the references made in these chapters to the political situation of the period. Why do you think that Barstow makes these references (or causes his characters to make them)?

3 'The way the reader sees – and understands – people and events is not always the same as the way in which Joby sees and understands.' Give some examples, and explanation, of such differences of outlook in these initial chapters.

Assignments

1 At the beginning of the novel Joby's mother goes into hospital, an event which causes anxiety and tension in the family. Describe – or imagine – a similar separation, not necessarily involving illness, in your family or one known to you. Try to bring out (and sympathize with) the different responses of each person.

2 Joby defends Snap in the face of mild bullying from Gus and his gang (Chapter 2). Describe, in dialogue form if you like, an occasion when you have defended, or been defended by, a friend under attack.

Chapter 4

Joby's 'education' in the ways of the world proceeds rapidly in this chapter. He is thrown out of the cinema, unjustly, by the attendant. The incident is small but the memory of it gnaws at Joby and he later (Chapter 9) attributes a series of misfortunes to this initial one. Mollie takes him to a wood where they spy on Agnes Macleod having sex. Joby is fascinated by the sight, without quite knowing why, and, egged on by Mollie, he joins her in some childish sexual display. Neither event is particularly important in itself, although each produces strong and uncomfortable feelings in Joby: he is 'consumed with anger and hatred' for the man who picks on him in the cinema; and later on he is ignorant and panicked enough to think that what he and Mollie have done together (in fact, nothing) is enough to produce a baby. Small incidents, but each offers a glimpse of features of life – injustice, powerlessness, sexuality – which the boy has not been required to understand until now.

Foundry Yard was the town's slum quarter As in *A Kind of Loving* a
clear distinction is drawn between the decent and respectable working-
class tradition (embodied in Joby's mother) and a squalid, feckless one.

Flash Gordon The famous, twenty-fifth-century space hero of several
film serials produced in the late 1930s. It is hardly necessary to add
that Flash's arch-enemy was the Emperor Ming.

He wasn't looking for a fight with anybody Joby is not aggressive or
quarrelsome, but he is ready to defend himself (or Snap).

every boy had to have a mother This piece of Joby's thinking niecely
catches the grudging acceptance by pre-pubescent boys of the place of
girls 'in the scheme of things'. Girls in themselves are no more than
inferior versions of boys – but they are needed to become mothers (of
boys, naturally). Such comments make convincing Barstow's unforced
re-creating of boyhood in *Joby*.

**'I'm not scared,' Joby said. 'I got thrown out of the pictures this
afternoon.'** Joby is, of course, alarmed and embarrassed at what
Mollie suggests. He tries to change the subject and to assert his
toughness by claiming to have done what he was in fact innocent of
(shooting pellets in the cinema). The false accusation filled him with
resentment and a sense of injustice: ironically, he now brandishes the
same accusation to impress the girl.

Chapter 5

The second half of Joby's Saturday, and the low point in his
spirits. The fight with Gus is the culmination of a group of
disturbing encounters or events (the quarrel with the cinema
attendant, the spying on Agnes Macleod, etc.) and Joby looks
around for shelter and comfort. The main provider of these
things is his mother and, in her absence, his loneliness and worry
rise to such a pitch that he makes a desperate trip to the hospital
to see her.

It is Joby's isolation that is stressed throughout the chapter –
even Snap deserts him, afraid of the fight that will break out
between Joby and Gus. Joby reaches out towards the adult
world, for he needs 'a grown-up whom he could trust and who
would ... talk to him directly.' But the adult world seems to
grow larger, more frightening or indifferent, as Joby appeals to
it. His father is too preoccupied with his own worries to bother
about Joby. There is poignancy in the scene when Joby asks his
father whether he can stay to have tea in his own home; the boy
wants the consolation of familiar surroundings and the reassurance of good news about his mother, and Mr Weston remains
almost completely unresponsive to his son's urgent needs. Joby

has to explain, too, why he was thrown out of the cinema, he must give vent to his sense of injustice, but again the father seems – hurtfully – untroubled by everything his son says. The other adult figures who feature in this chapter are equally unsympathetic, even hostile. He is questioned in the hospital by a nurse whose mood he cannot interpret; panic-stricken, he runs from a hospital attendant ('the hand fell on his shoulder'); returning to his aunt's, he is greeted with fury and incomprehension.

Even the neutral environment of the hospital takes on frightening overtones, underlining Joby's isolation and helplessness, his *smallness*. Its great walls 'reared up', it has 'hundreds of windows'. Inside, the hall is described as 'a vast place' with a 'high vaulted ceiling' and 'high narrow windows'. There are also plaques on the walls which are too high for Joby to read. There is a portrait there, but it is of a mayor, the image of distant adult authority. No longer among his equals or in a comforting setting, Joby becomes a frightened, lost child, 'drunk with grief'.

The tablecloth had stains on it The tiny detail suggests that Joby's father isn't that concerned with domestic order and tidiness.

'Is there a cricket match down in the field tonight?' Throughout the dialogue between Joby and his father, much is left unsaid – at least on the boy's part. We sense behind this question Joby's simple desire to communicate with his father, to remain in his company for as long as possible.

'sick-club dues' Subscription paid regularly into a fund which would support the wage-earner during illness (when he would not be paid by his employer). Mr Weston is possibly using this as an excuse for not keeping company with his son.

a small tear in the protective fabric of his world Joby now sees things differently (because he sees them through the 'tear' in the cocoon of childhood security and protection which his home has always provided before). The image is ambiguous in its implications. On the one hand, it implies that Joby is seeing things as they really are (without the benefit of a protective barrier), as he must learn to do; on the other, the phrase 'a small tear' hints at the spoiling of something previously whole and unflawed.

a great repair shop for human beings Another ambiguous phrase. To think of a hospital as a 'repair shop' may reassure only if people are considered in the same detached, slightly dehumanized light as cars (Joby sees the shortcomings of this image at the end of this paragraph). The comparison does, however, reinforce the boy's impression of the hospital as somewhere essentially inhospitable and frightening – not a place where people would choose to go.

a white unconscious face protruding from taut blankets The only patient Joby glimpses reminds him of the danger to his mother, powerless in the hands of people who 'didn't really care' (as Joby cared for her).

He wasn't going to bare himself now in front of Aunt Daisy Joby will not reveal his vulnerability to anyone (except his parents, and especially his mother). He keeps his silence and his dignity in the face of hostile or uncomprehending adults.

Chapter 6

Rebuffed by the grown-ups, Joby finds some comfort in being accepted by Gus and a member of his gang. It is perhaps significant that, encouraged by them, Joby disobeyes his aunt and plays innocent truant from the tedium of Sunday School by going to see the band playing in Cressley. Bossed about, misunderstood, or simply unwanted by adults, Joby looks for company and independence with people of his own age. The grown-up world, however, continues to present Joby with problematic situations: there is the behaviour of his father and Mona, which he witnesses but about which he says nothing (because he doesn't fully understand what is happening? because he does understand, and therefore preserves a tactful silence? because he has no one to tell such secret things to?). There is also the story of the suicide of Snap's uncle, as told to Joby by Gus. This leads to a splendidly realistic debate between the three boys on the best means of committing suicide, conducted with a kind of disinterested ghoulishness, but the question asked by Joby – 'Well . . . what did he want to do that for?' – goes unanswered; another baffling bit of adult activity, even if the boys view the suicide as providing an exciting talking-point.

a state of personal salvation from which the ommissions and shortcomings of others could be seen the more clearly Aunt Daisy is devout, not least in enforcing her principles on others. She has selected a form of religious observance which confirms her sense of moral superiority and priggish intolerance. She takes pleasure in condemning and finding fault. Joby cannot warm to or confide in her at this critical point in his life.

a Sunday shift, which was against Aunt Daisy's principles i.e. the principle that Sunday is set aside for rest and religious observance.

with more of irritation in his voice than anger Joby's father is less concerned with what his son has been doing than with the bother Joby might cause him by any misbehaviour.

'What's he want to be worried about her for?' The comment shows a profound lack of imagination and understanding. The father assumes his son has no right to be worried. He now uses the mother's being in hospital as a means of punishing Joby for 'upsetting' his aunt. He will worry his wife – and thereby increase Joby's sense of guilt – by telling her all about it. Joby sees there is something confused and vindictive in this adult position, which he can't put his finger on. The only person to show him any sympathy is Mona.

Joby wasn't so sure Snap was a mate of his now The beginning of the switch in Joby's allegiance to Gus.

it was very pleasant being accepted by Gus and Tommy Partly because Joby seems to have been abandoned by everyone else (family, Snap), partly because he half acknowledges Gus's strength as a leader and is gratified to be 'selected' by the other boy.

'Sly, underhand ways' Aunt Daisy's description of her nephew's behaviour is not only inappropriate (Joby had said nothing, not out of cunning, but because he feared the truth would make him vulnerable) but also revealing of her cold, rigorous personality.

Questions and assignments on Chapters 4–6

1 'Grown-ups – he hated them all.' (Chapter 5). Justify Joby's reaction by examining what happens to him in these chapters.

2 Provide a character sketch of Aunt Daisy. What view of her does the author encourage us to take?

Assignments

1 Describe an occasion when you have been unjustly told off or punished.

2 Write the letter that Joby might have sent to his mother in hospital (Chapter 6). Try to write 'in character'.

3 Write a dialogue between Snap and Joby on the subject of the uncle's suicide (such a conversation does not in fact occur in the novel). This could also be an improvised oral exercise. Again, use what you know about these two characters.

Chapter 7

This chapter deals with Joby's full initiation into Gus's circle and his discovery of the exciting (because dangerous) anti-adult activity of shop-lifting. Joby rationalizes what he is doing: stealing like this 'wouldn't hurt anybody'; it is part of the guerilla war waged by the boys against 'the world of grown-ups'. Like most people – children or adults – Joby is able to reject uncomfortable labels such as 'thief' by the simple device of believing that they could apply only to others but not himself. His motives and behaviour are exceptional, not to be judged by ordinary standards. He has further reasons for stealing: the activity confirms his place in Gus's group (and with his acceptance here comes an added status); there is also the sheer thrill of shop-lifting, offering 'a tension that seemed to charge his blood with electricity'.

Joby perhaps appears at his least sympathetic or engaging in this chapter. We understand how he is drawn, unwillingly at first, into the world of petty dishonesty held out by Gus and how his horror is replaced by fascination and excitement. The narrative doesn't condone or explicitly condemn at this point. The activities of Joby and his friends, most of them natural and harmless boyish pursuits, are simply recorded or dramatized. Nevertheless we do see that Joby has to go through various mental contortions to justify to himself what he is doing. And when Snap calls round to attempt to resume a friendship that has lapsed, Joby is uncomfortable. He no longer respects Snap, knows that Gus is 'contemptuous' of him, and senses that his old friend would not 'want to join in that [i.e. stealing] even if he were invited'. When Joby's mother again expresses her dislike of Snap, he is pleased because her attitude places another little barrier between himself and the boy whom Joby has come to identify 'almost . . . (as) his conscience'. In some sense, therefore, Joby knows he's not behaving well and is glad to be rid of the company of someone who might have pointed this out.

How did they touch upon her cosy world Perhaps because he is in company with more robust and 'realistic' boys Joby sees more clearly the gap between himself and Elsa. He no longer indulges in childish day-dreams in which he takes the role of hero.

His mother came home There is no description of the preparations for her return (if any) or the excitement that Joby presumably felt. The slightly throwaway quality of the sentence possibly suggests that his mother's absence, and her return, don't matter quite as much to Joby as they would have done before he discovered new activities with new friends. Things quickly get back to normal. With a child's resilience Joby rapidly forgets what he has been through while she has been away. **That was the kind of friend he was.** Feeling uncomfortable because he has dismissed Snap, Joby searches out his friend's failings so as to justify his own behaviour.

Chapter 8

Once again Joby finds himself in conflict with adult authority, but whereas earlier encounters had been marked by fear or resentment he feels, after their release by the shopkeeper who has caught them thieving, only an overwhelming sense of relief and gratitude. The crisis and the escape clear Joby's head. The only need now is to 'get as far away from Gus as possible'. The scene in the shop shows admirably Barstow's skilled handling of speech: the fierceness of the owner (more assumed than natural, it transpires); the glibness of Gus as he tries to explain away what they are doing; the panicked frankness of Joby, desperate to make a favourable impression by pointing out that he is to go to the Grammar School.

The chapter, like others in *Joby*, also provides glimpses of the lives, the habits and expectations of a northern working-class community half a century ago. There is a vivid evocation of the one week of respite offered to the workers when the town's industries closed down for the yearly seaside holiday. The community worked together, and enjoyed itself together. Joby's doubts as to whether his parents will be able to afford all the things he needs for his next school lead him to contemplate his good fortune in being permitted by them to go *at all*. Other parents have pushed their children out to work (at fourteen) or refused to consider the further education of a girl (on the grounds that such education was a 'waste'). These details are not only interesting in their own right, they also underline Joby's sense of precarious privilege. He is lucky in being allowed what is denied to others (an education!), and such thoughts are apt because they come just before a moment when it seems as though everything will be taken away from him. Caught in the shop, he sees a nightmarish trail of disgrace which will lead him to Borstal 'or somewhere just as bad'.

A grin of mingled admiration and unease Admiration at Gus's coolness and daring, unease because the other boy plainly hasn't 'learned his lesson' despite what he said to the shopkeeper. It's probably at this moment that Joby decides to have nothing more to do with Gus and his friends. He is no longer concerned with the gang-leader's opinion of him.

Chapter 9

Joby has to face 'the consequences of his misdeeds'. One crisis follows another. In a sense, these crises are not 'serious'. Over-hearing a conversation between his mother and their next-door neighbour, Joby misunderstands a reference to 'that Macleod lass' who is 'havin' a bairn'. He immediately thinks of Mollie and the time he spent with her after they spied on her sister. His ignorance is amusing – but Joby still suffers for it. His other venture with a girl, the sending of the letter and bottle of scent to Elsa Laedeker, also goes disastrously wrong. He has to account to his mother for his behaviour, and the guilt and shame that he experiences spring not from any moral assessment of his actions but from the much more immediate and powerful sensa-tion that he has injured his mother by what he's done. Accur-ately and convincingly, Barstow shows how, particularly in children, behaviour and conscience are moulded not by some abstract moral framework but by an awareness of the effect of our actions on those who matter to us. Joby loves his mother, and when she is distressed by what he has done 'his heart yearned towards her'. Having confessed some of the truth and been punished, he feels 'almost happy', because he hopes that everything will be restored to normal between himself and his parents. Much as he may distrust and resent the adult world on occasions, Joby also has a strong need – like most children – for its affection and approval.

But the world of the grown-ups has its own problems, ones not to be so easily resolved as Joby's. The relationship betwen Mr Weston and Mona, glimpsed and scarcely comprehended by the boy, comes into the open. Joby eavesdrops on the confrontation between his mother and Aunt Daisy, who in her self-righteous fashion is determined that her sister should know the full extent of her husband's 'misbehaviour'. She takes so much pleasure in squeezing out the details of the scandal from her daughter and indulging in a little feast of condemnation that Joby's mother, isolated and defensive, at last loses patience with her priggish superiority. One of the most touching scenes in the novel occurs when Joby enters the darkened living-room where his mother is still sitting. Joby wants reassurance – is his father going to return home? – but he also wants to offer something to his mother, to atone for the worry he's caused her, to re-establish their intimacy. Hesitantly, he apologizes for 'the scent an' all that'. The scene is understated, the dialogue spare, but we sense behind it the weight of the feelings bearing down on mother and son.

ether Anaesthetic gas used in operations.

one or two points he thought Snap might have been able to clear up for him It is significant that Joby considers returning to Snap in his confusion.

Coral Island Famous boys' adventure story by the Victorian writer, R. M. Ballantyne (1825–94). Its popularity lasted well into this century. Joby has a favourite (grisly) passage which, because it makes him realize his comparative good fortune, he reads when he needs cheering up.

Somehow he thought the troublemakers were not all wicked Joby's reflections on human behaviour are, inevitably, a bit straightforward and limited – it's the first time he's ever thought about such things – but already he has reached a more subtle and tolerant position than that occupied by, say, his Aunt Daisy, who would take pleasure in pointing out that troublemakers were, by definition, evil and to be condemned.

'whited sepulchre' i.e. a hypocrite (the phrase is from St Matthew's gospel and points to the external purity and cleanness of the tomb, or sepulchre, which hides what's rotten inside).

'Why, I've never heard such talk in my life.' Aunt Daisy's indignation springs from her sister's having hit on the truth: she *is* enjoying the scene in a way.

He still couldn't make out what had happened One of the times when the reader's understanding is distinct from Joby's. His bafflement here suggests his innocence, as does his earlier fear that he was responsible for Mollie's expecting a child. Though ignorant of the detail, Joby nevertheless feels the emotional consequences of what has occurred: his mother's fear, his own anxiety that his father will not return.

humbug Fake, hypocritical talk.

Chapter 10

Joby began with the departure of Joby's mother into hospital, and the breaching of the ring of security which had until that moment surrounded Joby's life. The novel ends with the return of the father to the home, and it is his son's heartfelt appeal that causes Mr Weston to come back. There is nothing calculated in what Joby does, nor is there any sentimentality in the narrative. As in *A Kind of Loving*, the end to *Joby* is not really conclusive, and is not meant to be so. The family's problems are not solved. Joby's parent's are restored to him, partly through his own actions, but the simplicity and invulnerability of childhood can never be regained. In a key moment Joby has 'for the first time a sense of his father as not his father', when he sees him sitting alone on the river bank. Any child perceives its parents only in relation to itself – they have no real, independent existence as human beings. The realization that parents have their own history, preoccupations, weaknesses – in short, that they, like their children, are 'only' human, with all that that entails – may be for the child a late realization as well as an unwelcome one. But it is, of course, a necessary part of the progress towards adulthood. Joby does not see this all at once; rather, he has 'a vague sense' of his father's life being detached from his own, stretching 'back to a time and a life before he himself was born'. But the sight of his father, detached in this way from himself, from his family, indeed from any company at all, provokes in Joby a kind of pitying curiosity. The sudden awareness of the separateness of his father's life – and, by implication, his own separateness from his father – is a proper milestone in Joby's growth; it also enables him to appeal directly to his father, to urge his return home, because he can speak as one anxious, forlorn person to another: 'Oh, come on home with me, Dad. It'll be all right. Me mam's waiting for you.'

He wondered if he had done the right thing Joby has pretended to be unable to read the old lady's letter because he doesn't want to deal with the distress its contents would cause her. Later, he analyses his motives quite shrewdly. The episode is placed between the crisis in Joby's own family and its partial resolution at the end of the novel. It perhaps serves as a reminder that whatever has occurred to his parents is not the worst that could have happened (the letter brings news of a death). It is not necessary, however, to search for some 'point' in this episode; Joby is confronted by a situation which tests him and which he – very naturally – evades.

Joby's mother was wearing her pride. She will defend her husband, even though she has been badly hurt by his behaviour, against the inquisitive malice of her sister's family.

It would be easy now to feel proud that he had spared the old lady
Joby is learning to be clear-sighted about what he does. He doesn't
deceive himself (as he did over the shop-lifting escapades).

**the next question . . . could hardly have entered his mind before he
experienced the sight of his father sitting alone** It takes the shock of
perceiving his father as a separate individual (a man instead of a
parent) to make Joby put into words his partial awareness of
everything he has witnessed over the past few weeks. Because his
father is someone with his own private thoughts and feelings, as Joby
realizes, he can therefore make choices; and the choice that matters to
his son – the only question – is, 'D'you like our Mona better than me
mam?' Joby has the 'child's' privilege of being entitled to ask direct and
simple questions.

'She'll be wondering where *you* are' His father has sunk so low in his
own self-esteem that he can't conceive that his wife would be worried
about his whereabouts, only Joby's.

'Oh, come on home with me, Dad.' The intense relief of finding that
his father is safe enables Joby to say what he was earlier unable to
voice. All that matters is that family solidarity is restored, in the face of
opposition if necessary ('You don't care about me Auntie Daisy an'
them, do you? They don't matter to us, do they?'). And it is Joby who is
chiefly responsible for bringing Mr Weston back, by displaying so
openly his need for his father's return.

He couldn't see it, but he knew it was there. Riding home on his
father's shoulders (a reversion to an earlier childhood treat), Joby
finds trust and confidence coming back to him. After all the threats to
family unity – his mother's going to hospital, his own and his father's
actions – they have still survived intact. The last sentence of the novel
has a simple eloquence.

Questions and assignments on Chapters 7–10

1 Trace the growth of Joby's involvement in stealing from
shops. How and why does he come to realize that what he is
doing is wrong?

2 Which character(s) do you sympathize with in the scene
(Chapter 9) when Mrs Weston is confronted by her sister with
the evidence of the relationship between her husband and her
niece? Give reasons for your response.

3 How satisfactory do you find the end of the novel? Explain
your response.

Assignments

1 'If only they could go back ten minutes . . .' Joby desperately wishes when they have been caught shoplifting. It's a common enough wish after some disaster; write about a time when you have experienced it.

2 Write the dialogue that occurs between Mr and Mrs Weston after the husband returns home at the end of the novel. Joby might take part. This could also be an oral exercise. Base your interpretations of the characters on what they do and say in the last couple of chapters (for example, it is easy to see that Joby's father is shamefaced about the whole incident. How would he handle this uncomfortable reunion?).

Stan Barstow's art in *Joby*

Like *A Kind of Loving*, *Joby* is deceptively simple in its content and style. The later novel does not have the diffuse colloquial style of Barstow's first novel but it shares with it a clarity, plainness and vigour in the narrative, hallmarks of this writer. The style of each novel is appropriate to its narrator or subject matter: chatty and relaxed in *A Kind of Loving*, because we are given the impression that we are listening to the private, unedited thoughts of Vic Brown; compact and lucid in *Joby*, because Barstow is intent on capturing something of the innocent clear-sightedness of a child's view of the world.

The narrative of *Joby* is uncomplicated. At the beginning Joby's mother goes into hospital; he worries about her absence; he falls out with an old friend and in with a new, faintly disreputable gang of boys; his father and cousin Mona are involved in a half-hearted relationship which Aunt Daisy attempts to present in a scandalous light. There are other incidents, most of which follow on from these facts. At the end everything turns out 'all right' – in a way. Joby's family is restored to him. Outwardly the world is unchanged. But Joby himself has been altered by what has happened, and more so than he perhaps realizes at the time. The story is simple enough, and not without drama (see, for example, the scene where Joby is caught shop-lifting or the one where he eavesdrops on his mother and aunt), but its significance lies not so much in the detail as in the universal elements it contains.

A Kind of Loving describes Vic Brown's coming to terms with a world of responsibility and compromise, unsatisfactory but ine-scapable in its demands. He has to change. Joby, too, must change, although not in so self-conscious and painful a fashion. Joby, like any child, has to go through a period of adjustment in his perception and understanding of the adult world, particularly that part closest to him, his parents. By the end of the novel, he sees his mother and father not as everlasting protectors but as people who can hurt, or be hurt. This does not entail any lessening of love or need. Indeed, at the end, Joby voices explicitly the need he – and his mother – have for the father's return. But side by side with this acknowledgement of renewed love comes the sensation of pity, the awareness of others' vulnerability – on the river bank Joby sees not his father 'but a man, sitting alone with his world pulled about him like a cloak'. The father is as isolated as the son, perhaps more so, because his guilt is harder to get rid of. Of course, Joby does not see this change clearly for himself, and on the closing page he reverts willingly to a child-like status (he is carried on his father's shoulders). It is this change, however, which the novel is principally concerned with, *the change from childhood reliance to adolescent uncertainty*. Joby is not quite so sure of things by the end of the novel but such unsureness, or insecurity, is an unavoidable aspect of growth.

It is part of the subtlety of *Joby* that just as its central character is moving from childhood to maturity, so too does the viewpoint of the novel occupy a middle ground between the outlook of a child and that of an adult. Almost everything that happens is seen through Joby's eyes (there are a few exceptions, all imparting information required by the reader in following the narrative). Because we see as the child sees, the vision is often partial or lop-sided. Joby witnesses, but doesn't fully understand, something of what takes place between his father and Mona. When he goes to the hospital he is intimidated, overwhelmed by the place, and no attempt is made to insert an adult perspective here. To these and other situations an adult would react differently. Often we are invited to 'read between the lines'. We understand much more quickly than Joby what is happening between Mr Weston and his niece (or is it that the adult mentality is merely more suspicious and knowing than the child's?). As a minor example of where the reader's understanding is different, almost contrary, to Joby's, look at the scene in Chapter 2 in which Joby and his friend Snap encounter the frightening Gus and his gang. It is obvious that Snap is looking for a way out; but Joby's admiration for his friend is such that he doesn't notice the other's timidity, even though he is conscious of his own. In this and other instances the reader stands a bit higher than Joby and can see a little further. None of this reduces our identification with the central character. We sympathize with him partly because of his predicament, partly because there are universal aspects to what he goes through (we have all been children), and partly because of the very nature of the book itself. *Joby* is not a childhood memoir, a sequence of events recollected in nostalgic tranquillity. It is a novel, a re-creation of what it was like to be a particular child in a certain place and time. As such, *Joby* engages us directly, it does not stand detached or aloof from the boy at its centre.

It should be apparent from what I have said above that the novel is on Joby's side. Our sympathies rarely, if ever, leave him. A child, in fiction, is easily made sympathetic: he or she is usually passive in relation to the adult world, possibly bullied by it, neglected, and so on. By the same token it is very easy to be sentimental in the re-creation of childhood. Barstow avoids this trap. The reader's feelings are not manipulated. Joby's problems are not presented as exceptional, nor is his response to them. He is average; he is a follower rather than a leader; he finds excuses for himself or runs away, if he can. After he gets thrown out of the cinema, we are told that he 'was no angel and he had made his share of mischief'. The very ordinariness of the central character adds to the narrative validity and appeal.

If *Joby* is pro-child, so to speak, it also manages to be on the side of the adults – or most of them. Given that almost every-thing is seen as it is experienced by Joby, and given his frequent misunderstanding of or hostility to grown-ups, it is remarkable that tolerance and warmth (also marks of Barstow's writing) are extended to the adult world too. This comes across most clearly in the characterization of Mr and Mrs Weston. Joby's mother emerges, largely through dialogue, as a proud, dignified, some-what embattled figure, the 'heart' of the household (like Vic's mother in *A Kind of Loving*). It is harder to appreciate Mr Weston; evasive, morose, at some moments a rather feeble figure, he has very little about him that is attractive. Yet, because we see him – in his solitariness and failure – through the lens of Joby's own love and need he becomes an indispensable member of the family, someone to be accepted not condemned. Other adult figures show themselves to be more responsive than a child expects: the nurse who questions Joby at the hospital, the shop-keeper who he at first thinks will call the police; others again are frail or vulnerable: the old lady who asks Joby to read the letter from her son; the hapless Mona, the one person to sense some-thing of what Joby is going through while his mother is away. The only character to appear consistently unattractive is Aunt Daisy. Self-righteous and unloving, she has a well-developed capacity for spreading discomfort and misery around her.

General questions on *A Kind of Loving* and *Joby*

1 What are the advantages and disadvantages of the first-person narration in *A Kind of Loving*?

Guideline answer

First-person narration immediately makes claims on the reader for his attention, interest, sympathy. It is a rejection by the novelist of impersonal or detached mode of narrative, and an invitation to the reader to be the attentive, 'silent' partner in a kind of dialogue. Barstow's – or rather, Vic's – style has the tone (casual, colloquial) of someone talking to a very close friend; his problems and pleasures almost become our own. We have a sense of 'privilege' at eavesdropping on his most private moments, and so always feel a residual sympathy for him even when he's condemned by other characters. Speaking in the first person Vic can 'explain' himself, without appearing to apologize or justify himself, because this form of narrative (like a soliloquy in stage play) seems to be 'spoken' only for the benefit of the teller, not to convince the outside world. As examples, take those scenes where Vic appears at his most selfish or insensitive (when Ingrid first informs him she's pregnant, when he drunkenly confronts his mother-in-law), and see how differently we would respond if events were narrated from a different viewpoint. Because we are *'inside'* the character we can appreciate his frustration, confusion, helplessness, etc. as we could never appreciate them from the exterior. Vic's story is outwardly very ordinary – young man gets caught up in relationship, pregnancy, 'shotgun' wedding, and so on – and its interest must come not so much from what happens as *who* it happens to. Therefore, the personality of the narrator, his inner life, is all-important. A disadvantage of first-person narration is the limited viewpoint – story-teller's horizons are limited (he can't see into others' hearts and minds or be in two places at once, as the all-seeing, all-knowing novelist can). *A Kind of Loving* might be told from several points of view; the author could step forward and explain things (as he does on occasions in *Joby*). But it's hardly necessary to add that it would be a very different book: more 'balanced', 'fairer' perhaps in its treatment of some of the characters, but altogether lacking the edge – immediate, jagged, apparently artless – which the first-person narration gives to it.

2 How significant is the fact that *A Kind of Loving* is set in the late 1950s? To what extent does this affect the course of events in the novel?

3 What role do Vic's parents play in the novel?

4 'Ingrid is the real victim in the story.' Discuss.

5 Explain why work plays such a prominent part in *A Kind of Loving* and comment on the attitudes of different characters towards it.

6 How far would you agree that Vic Brown is a man of mixed, even contradictory, qualities?

7 '*A Kind of Loving* must be a one-sided story – everything is seen from the man's point of view.' Comment.

8 If you were adapting *A Kind of Loving* for the stage or the cinema, which episodes would you choose to dramatize? Each medium has different requirements. Give reasons for the selection you make.

9 There are other marriages in the novel apart from Vic and Ingrid's (the two sets of parents, Vic's sister and brother-in-law). How are they compared and contrasted with Vic and Ingrid's 'kind of loving'?

10 'I'm like thousands of others' – why does Barstow make his central characters so ordinary?

11 How does Barstow achieve a 'documentary' feel in *A Kind of Loving* so that we have the illusion that we are reading about what really occurred?

12 How effective is the use of the present tense and a colloquial style in *A Kind of Loving*? Use examples.

13 Barstow has been described as a regional novelist. What aspects of *A Kind of Loving* and *Joby* could support this description?

14 Why do you think Barstow sets *Joby* in the months immediately preceding the outbreak of the Second World War?

15 'At the end of their stories both Joby and Vic Brown have grown up.' Comment, in relation to one or both of the central characters.

16 *Joby* reminds us how much time children spend watching what adults do, even if they don't fully understand their behaviour. Find and discuss some examples of this in the novel.

17 In what ways does *Joby* seem to you to evoke a vanished world? In what ways is his world the same as yours?

18 'Change, individual or social, is important in both novels.' Discuss, with reference to one or both books.

19 Comment on some of the distinctive features of Barstow's style in *A Kind of Loving* or *Joby*.

20 What have you gained from reading either (or both) of these books?